Advanced Praise For:

Performance Eating: The High Performance High School Athlete Nutrition Guide

"Jones's book is a must-read for any serious dancer. In the black hole of nutrition and fitness books, **Performance Eating: The High Performance High School Athlete Nutrition Guide** is a like bright star on Broadway. Jones's message is simple and straightforward. He helps you understand the "why" without getting too technical or mind-numbing."

Ann Reinking, Tony Award winning Choreographer

"This book takes the guesswork out of muscle fueling. Information is condensed and you can start on any chapter you want. Whether you're a soccer player, cyclist, football player, or marching band member this book is a must for your performance library. This book will give you the secrets of the pros."

Julio Llanos, MS, ATC, Head Trainer Columbus State University

"This book includes the information you need to build more strength, lean muscle mass, in less time than ever before. The methods are safe, natural, can be used by anyone from beginning exercisers to professional athletes. This book is not a gimmick. This is the future of high school athletic sports nutrition and performance."

Elizabeth Martin (www.eamartin.com)
Executive and leadership trainer, Former Director of Medical Services Atlanta
Olympic Games

D1041917

"I've been asked many times to recommend a good book on sports nutrition that's reliable and understandable. This is the one! It also includes a goal setting chapter and a motivational chapter…each of which is worth the price of the book itself. Devour this book as you would your food!"

Lance Kelly, MS, PT, ATC, Physical Therapist and personal trainer to professional, collegiate, and high school athletes

"William Jones, a physical therapist, nutrition and fitness expert, shows his knowledge of nutrition and sport far exceeds his peers. *Performance Eating: The High Performance High School Nutrition Guide* is unique in that it is written by someone who has the education but also the personal experience to match. Very often, people will write about subjects they may have studied, yet have little to no personal or practical experience. This is not the case with Jones. As a former bodybuilder turned martial artist turned marathoner he lives his advice. I greatly recommend this book to anyone who is an athlete and to those who work with athletes. It is a MUST for everyone's bookshelf."

Jurgen Cowling, PT (www.healinghands.us) President Healing Hands Physical Therapy Centers

Performance Eating

Performance Eating

✦

The High Performance High School Athlete Nutrition Guide

William Jones, MS, PT

iUniverse, Inc.
New York Lincoln Shanghai

Performance Eating
The High Performance High School Athlete Nutrition Guide

iUniverse books may be ordered through booksellers or by contacting:

iUniverse
2021 Pine Lake Road, Suite 100
Lincoln, NE 68512
www.iuniverse.com
1-800-Authors (1-800-288-4677)

Remember, before undertaking any nutritional and/or exercise program one should consult a physician. The Food and Drug Administration have not reviewed this material. This information is not intended to diagnose, treat, cure, or prevent any disease. This information is not intended to substitute for the services of trained health care professionals but is provided for general educational purposes only. Any nutritional opinions stated are based solely on personal experiences and research. Everyone is different. Therefore it is always recommended that before doing anything you first check with your personal physician to make sure any changes you create will work with your current medical condition and history.

If you do not wish to be bound by the above please return the book.

ISBN-13: 978-0-595-38740-3 (pbk)
ISBN-13: 978-0-595-83122-7 (ebk)
ISBN-10: 0-595-38740-3 (pbk)
ISBN-10: 0-595-83122-2 (ebk)

Printed in the United States of America

"To eat is a necessity, but to eat intelligently is an art."
—Francois La Rochefoucauld

Contents

Acknowledgments

I'd like to thank all the people who have ever asked me questions. Their questions spurred me on to either look up the answers or to ask people who are smarter than me. I'd also like to thank those smarter people who answered my questions!

This brings me to my parents. I asked. They answered. Some answers were better than others. Some were right. Some were right at the time. It was a great ground for higher-level thinking.

Thanks to all that helped add to this endeavor:

Dennise Brogdon, my editor. Without her this would still be tucked away in my computer under some obscure file name.

Bill Kazmaier, Worlds Strongest Man and ESPN commentator. Great guy on and off the platform. One of the most motivating persons I have ever met.

Julio Llanos, present head trainer at Columbus State University and former head trainer to Fort Valley State University. It's only a matter of time before he's with the pros.

Elizabeth Martin, (www.eamartin.com). What can I say about Elizabeth? A lot! From a professional standpoint she is a physical therapist, has been on faculty at Emory University, was the first woman in Olympic history to serve as director of medical services at the Atlanta Olympic Games and is a former CEO of the Georgia Chapter Arthritis Foundation. She now lends her experience and expertise to provide leadership development and executive coaching to professionals ready to control their future. As she says *"The best way to predict the future is to create it."* She certainly has helped me with mine!

Lance Kelly, physical therapist and personal trainer to professional athletes (NFL, NBA, WNBA, LPGA, and MLB), collegiate and high school athletes.

Ann Reinking, director, choreographer, performer, dancer, and Tony Award winner for "Chicago". A totally gifted and grounded person that exemplifies the concept of giving.

Jurgen Cowling, physical therapist and President of Healing Hands Physical Therapy Centers. Just an all around great therapist and someone who continually improves himself and his centers.

Much appreciation to the "group": Darryl, Bonnie, Mike S., Babette, Joe, and Krista.

Thanks to Rick, Mike, Joe. Just 'cuz.

And to Helen, with much gratitude and appreciation, the person who gives me the highest level of support no matter how outlandish my ideas seem to be.

Foreword

Why I am recommending this book? Simple. I believe the contents of this book may be the most valuable information you will ever discover for making smart choices about athletic nutrition. This book will help you create a nutritional road map toward maximum sports performance regardless of your sport.

Many books have been written about exercise and nutrition. The author is an experienced sports medicine physical therapist and sports nutritionist who has actually been on the field, in the dojo and in the weight room. This book is the *real thing.* It is based on scientific facts and practical experience.

I feel this book represents the best nutritional tool available today for high school athletes and college athletes as well. It is a must read for any one interested in physical fitness and performance. It is easy to understand and written as if the author is talking to you. Not at you. Not down to you. But to you. The book won't bore you with a lot of pictures and graphs you won't even look at. You've already seen a lot of pictures of people lifting weights, running or drinking sports drinks. This book will not waste your time with that. There are plenty of other ones that will.

Athletes are always looking for the "magic supplement" or the "secret" training concept that will enhance performance. Despite the wealth of information regarding nutrition there has always been a cloud of controversy over the athletic dinner table. The misconceptions of feeding the body for performance always brings up a boatload of questions: What foods and fluids are the best choices before, during and after training? How can I best recover from my exercises? Can nutrition allow me to train harder and longer without injury? These questions are answered here.

Whether you're a distance runner, a weight trainer, a dancer, cheerleader, or even in the marching band this book will show you how to achieve your best performance. If you are a serious competitor using the ideas in this book will have a dramatic impact on your success as an athlete.

Professional teams usually have a team nutritionist that works with the strength and conditioning coach to develop individualized nutrition programs. Unfortunately a professional and personal nutritionist is the luxury very few athletes can afford. *This book is your personal nutritionist.*

I am excited about this book because it gives athletes at the high school and college level an equalizer to the pros.

I hope you'll enjoy this book is much as I have. I only wish I could have had this book when I was in high school.

Bill Kazmaier
Worlds Strongest Man
ESPN Commentator

P.S. Train hard and hit the books harder.

Introduction: How Do You Use this Book?

You don't have to read this book from cover to cover—it isn't algebra. One chapter doesn't build on the last one. The book is designed for you to read what you want. Read the chapters that best represent your sport. Read the others to increase you knowledge and to pass information on to others. Write in the book. Use an accent marker for lines you wish to remember. It's yours. Do whatever you need to get the most out of it.

I sometimes address athletes, coaches, and parents on the role that nutrition plays in enhancing sports performance. Afterwards I'm barraged by a boatload of questions from the audience. What's the best thing to eat? How? When? How much water should I drink? Should I even drink water? Is beer appropriate for carbohydrate loading? (I'm serious!)

These questions show there is a gap between nutrition in the lab and on the playing field. Some people get too little information, some people get too much information, some people get dated information, some people get wrong information and some get conflicting information. It can be confusing. A lot of people get way too much information from magazines. They sometimes write about products that promise the world. I attended a seminar many years ago given by a former Mr. Universe. He told the audience that magazines may have only 5% of good advice the rest was pure bull. The key is how to see through the bull.

For the parents of young athletes there is mostly a lack of information. Most general nutrition articles that appear in the media may not be appropriate for the special needs of teenage athletes. Some popular nutritional fads such as low carbohydrate diets may be detrimental to teenage athletic performance and growth.

Most professional teams usually have a nutritionist to develop individualized nutrition programs. Unfortunately a personal nutritionist is the luxury very few people can afford. As Bill Kazmaier has written: This book is your personal nutritionist.

This book provides simple and effective information for the high performance high school athlete. In order to accommodate for each sport's unique requirements, some examples from each sport are included in this book.

The nutrition methods described in this book will not turn you into a world champion by itself. There is much more that goes into a successful athletic performance. Nutrition, training, commitment, genetics, talent, coaching, and motivation are all essential factors. Whatever your level of athletic performance the nutrition information described in this book will help you reach your full potential.

At the end of each chapter you'll find the Performance Eating Wrap Up or "PE Wrap". Just an extremely brief summary.

This book based on current research. Research changes. For many years it was said that soy protein had a positive effect on heart health. The most recent research finds that it does not. This does not mean that soy protein is not healthy. It is. However it is an illustration at how our knowledge continues to change with the results of continued research.

Poor nutritional habits and inactivity contribute to about 310,000 to 580,000 deaths each year according to the U.S. Department of Health and Human Services Web site. That number exceeds the number of deaths from guns, drug use, or car accidents. Specifically, smoking and obesity are the two leading causes of death according to the Centers for Disease Control (CDC). Essentially, the two leading killers in the U.S. are choices people make. Your success depends on your choices. If you choose to be an athlete, choose to maximize your potential and stay healthy.

I didn't have a book like this available when I was in high school. Those were the barbaric days of no water during practice (to make us tougher), a lot of salt tablets, and sharing mouth pieces (I kid you not!).

Things have changed a lot since then. Some for the worse and some for the better. This book represents the better.

"If you care at all, you'll get some results. If you care enough, you'll get incredible results."
—Jim Rohn

The Macs: Carbohydrates, Fats, and Protein

"Man does not live by bread alone..."
—Matthew 4:4

The food you eat is divided into three main groups called macronutrients. The MACS. The macronutrients are carbohydrates, fats, and protein. Your body needs some of all three to function normally. As an athlete, your nutritional needs are different than the average person.

CARBOHYDRATES

Many years ago, bodybuilders were eating low carbohydrate and high protein diets. They did well with this type of diet. However, they did much better when they found that adding carbohydrates helped to increase the intensity of their workouts as well as spared their hard earned muscle.

After more nutritional research, high carb, medium to low protein diets became popular. A few years ago, high protein diets became popular again and carbohydrates once again became the evil nutrient. Carbohydrates aren't all good or all bad. They are an essential part of any champion athletes' diet.

Carbohydrates provide the athlete with fuel for training and proper body function. The best sources of carbohydrates include fruits, vegetables, and whole grains.

What are carbohydrates?

Carbohydrates come from a wide variety of foods (bread, butterbeans, popcorn, potatoes, cookies, pasta, corn, cake, and pie). The most common are sugars, fibers, and starches. Sugar is the basic building block of a carbohydrate. Basically, after you eat carbohydrates they are broken down into sugars (glucose) for the body to use. Fiber can't be broken down well and passes through the body (see the *Listen to Your Grandmother* chapter).

Carbohydrates are grouped into two categories: simple and complex. Simple carbohydrates include fruit sugar (fructose), corn or grape sugar (dextrose or glucose), and table sugar (sucrose). Basically, if you have an–ose at the end of the word, you've got yourself a sugar. Simple carbohydrates are digested quickly. Other examples include fruits, fruit juice, milk, yogurt, honey, syrup, and sugar.

Complex carbohydrates consist of three or more linked sugars, which mean they take longer to digest and are usually packed with fiber, vitamins and minerals. Examples are vegetables, cereals, legumes (peas and beans) and pasta. Simple carbohydrates were at one time considered bad and complex carbohydrates good, but this is not always the case.

Carbohydrates and the glycemic index

Explaining carbohydrates and the glycemic index makes the whole topic of carbohydrates a little more complicated, but only a little. A new system for classifying foods, the glycemic index, measures how fast and how far blood sugar rises after you eat.

An example of a high glycemic carbohydrate is white bread. White bread is converted quickly and raises the blood sugar. Brown rice is a low glycemic index example. It is digested slowly, which causes a lower and gentle blood sugar rise.

Diets with a lot of high-glycemic foods are associated with an increased risk for diabetes and heart disease. Diets with lower glycemic index foods are shown to help control type 2 diabetes.

Seem complicated? Simply put, try replacing highly processed foods with less processed whole-grain products. The whole subject of glycemic index and glycemic load (another topic) is beyond the scope of this book. If you want more information, there are many web sites and books devoted to this topic. (Check out the *Stuff You Don't Need* chapter.)

How much carbohydrate should you eat?

Don't worry. Unless you are on a low-carb and high-protein diet you won't have a problem. Experts recommend 50 to 60% of the total calories you eat should come from carbohydrates.

There is evidence that low-carbohydrate diets can help people lose weight. However, this is true with any calorie-restrictive plan. It's just a matter of staying on the plan. One problem with the low-carb diets is the potentially large amounts of fat involved. Since your body (and brain) favors carbohydrates for fuel no athlete should be on a low-carbohydrate diet.

This is your brain on carbohydrates.

Guess what is the primary fuel for your brain to function? Glucose. And glucose is easily converted from carbohydrates. It's estimated that your brain needs at least 130 grams of carbohydrates a day to function optimally. Research suggests carbohydrate feedings designed to increase blood glucose during training can improve both mental and physical function.

PE Carb Wrap

Eat them!

FAT

Fats are one of the macronutrients that supply calories to the body. (*Fat* is also the name of an album by a punk band called *The Descendents* from the early '80s. It's also a record label. FAT is used by a computer operating system to keep track of which clusters are allocated to specific files and which are available for use. But none of these matter here.)

Your body needs fat, but not an enormous amount. Fats are a necessary part of your diet. Your body uses fats for energy (calories), vitamin absorption, insulation, and protection. Fats are the most concentrated source of calories in your diet. Fats provide nine calories of energy per gram. Proteins and carbohydrates each provide four calories per gram. This is a very important topic to understand, not only for performance, but also for calorie counting and general health. Fats provide the *essential* fatty acids. Essentially, this means they are not made by the body and must be obtained from food.

Cholesterol

Cholesterol can be both good and bad; therefore, it's important to learn what cholesterol is and how to manage your cholesterol levels. Cholesterol is a fatty substance found naturally in animal foods, such as meat, fish, poultry, eggs, and dairy products. The body also produces cholesterol. Cholesterol is important for making hormones, for helping to manufacture vitamin D, and for building cell membranes. Cholesterol makes up about ten percent of the dry weight of brain tissue. It is essential to nutrition; therefore, the liver and brain make a little each day to insure you get enough. However, too much cholesterol can cause a build up on the artery walls and can slow the flow of blood.

Cholesterol travels in the bloodstream in *lipoproteins*. There are two types of lipoproteins. Low-density lipoproteins (LDL or *bad* cholesterol) deliver cholesterol to the body. High-density lipoproteins (HDL or *good* cholesterol) take cholesterol out of the bloodstream. High LDL cholesterol levels can contribute to heart disease.

There is evidence that buildup on the arteries begins in childhood and gets worse with time and it can lead to heart disease. Coronary heart disease, responsible for nearly half a million deaths annually, is the single leading cause of death in the U.S.

Total cholesterol levels for ages 2 to 19 years old should follow these numbers:
Acceptable—less than 170
Borderline—170 to 199
High—200 or higher.

Get your number from your doctor at your next physical. Think of this as an investment in your life.

Are all fats the same?

Nope, not all fats are created equal. Unless you have been living under a rock you ought to know eating too much fat can increase your risk of heart disease, increase your body weight (in a bad way), and decrease your performance. Not to mention, fats can increase the inches around your waist.

The bad fat.

To me, bad fat is the fat that's around my waist, which tends to get bigger during winter when I wear more clothes and workout less. However, we're talking about saturated fats and not my waistline.

Bad fats are found mainly in animal products such as butter, cheese, milk, ice cream, egg yolks, seafood, as well as meat and poultry skin. (Once I actually saw a kid eat a chicken-skin sandwich. That's right, a chicken-skin sandwich! He looked so happy, I had to try one. Tasty, but unhealthy! Don't try this at home!) Some vegetable fats like coconut oil, cocoa butter, palm kernel oil, and palm oil are also high in saturated fats. An excessive amount of fat can increase the risk of heart disease and stroke. (Am I driving that home yet?)

The badder fat!

I know, like we need to have another bad thing to eat. Trans-fatty acids (TFA) are found in small amounts of animal products. Heating liquid vegetable oils in the presence of hydrogen (called *hydrogenation*) also creates trans-fatty acids. The more hydrogenated the oil, the harder it is at room temperature. Therefore, a softer, easy spreading tub of margarine is less hydrogenated than a stick of margarine. Research suggests *partially hydrogenated vegetable oils* provide about three-fourths of the trans-fatty acids in the American diet.

Most of these fats are found in margarines, snack foods, and processed foods. They are often added to processed foods to increase the shelf life. Fried foods, like French fries, doughnuts, corn dogs, and onion rings, also contain a lot of trans fat. Be careful at the county fairs and carnivals!

Trans fats are worse than saturated fats because they raise bad LDL and lower good HDL. You should limit your saturated fat intake and try to eliminate your trans fats, altogether.

The good fat.

Believe it or not boys and girls, there is a good fat. These fats are considered good because they can improve your blood cholesterol levels.

Unsaturated fats come from plant sources, such as vegetable oils, nuts, and seeds. The main categories are polyunsaturated fats (found in sunflower, corn, and soybean oils) and monounsaturated fats (found in canola, peanut, and olive oils).

Other types of polyunsaturated fats are referred to as Omega-3 and Omega-6 fatty acids. Oil-rich fish and supplements, such as fish oil and cod liver oil (yuk) are good sources of polyunsaturated fats. Omega-3 fatty acids are considered *essential* because they are necessary but the body can't make them. They must be obtained from your diet. It is believed that the Omega-3s have anti-inflammatory benefits and help prevent heart disease. Omega-6s are said to lower blood cholesterol and support the skin. The American Heart Association recommends eating fish at least a couple times a week. Fish is a good source of protein and isn't high in saturated fat like beef. *Fatty* fish include mackerel, herring, sardines, albacore tuna and salmon. Also, soybeans, canola oil, walnuts, and flaxseed oil are good sources of polyunsaturated fats.

Atherosclerosis

Big word alert. When fatty material is deposited along the walls of arteries it is known as atherosclerosis. You may have heard it as hardening of the arteries. This fatty material may eventually block the arteries. Not a good thing. So why am I including this here? Research show it can begin early in life, as early as 3 years old. 1 out of 6 teenagers can have a degree of coronary artery disease. If you keep your fat intake and cholesterol levels low you have a better chance of not developing this disease over the years.

Fats and cancer

There is some discussion in the scientific community about the link between fats and cancer. Some studies show there are links and others do not. That being said, a diet high in fat is not going to help your performance or your looks.

How much should you eat?

The U.S. Department of Agriculture's 2005 Dietary Guidelines for Americans recommends keeping your intake of fat between 20% and 35% of your total daily calories. Of course, you should limit foods high in saturated fats and trans-fatty acids. Eat mostly polyunsaturated and monounsaturated fats. These are found in fish, nuts, and vegetable oils.

The hardest fats to watch out for are the trans fats. That's because they are in many different types of foods and aren't always listed on the label. The Food and Drug Administration (FDA) has required that all food labels list trans fats by January 1, 2006. Check the ingredients for *hydrogenated oils*. The closer these are to the front of the ingredient list, the more trans-fatty acids the food contains.

PE Fat Wrap

Watch out for the trans and saturated fats. Limit them in your diet. Eat the polys, monos, and Omegas.

> *"My favorite animal is steak."*—*Fran Lebowitz; Humorist, Essayist*

PROTEIN

What is it?

Protein is a substance made of a group of amino acids (It was also a punk group in the mid nineties out of San Francisco). Proteins are considered the *building blocks* of your body. There has been a lot of hype about protein over the past few years, but it's dieing down a bit now. Believe me; the controversy will be back again. It's almost like protein is the most important thing in the world to eat. It isn't. Muscles use carbohydrates as their primary energy source during competition or training, not protein.

However, protein is a necessary component of a healthy diet for athletes. It's just not the number one thing. There is no number one thing. You need some protein, some carbohydrates, and some fats. That is just the way your body works. Kinda like a car. It runs on gas, but without oil and the other fluids you won't get too far!

How much do you need?

During digestion, proteins are broken down into amino acids. The amino acids are used for the growth and repair of the body. It's been debated for a long time whether or not athletes need more protein than the average human. Well it's true; athletes do require more protein, but just slightly more.

Generally, athletes require about 0.5 to 1.0 grams per pound of bodyweight. Some authorities have upped the numbers just a little more to 1.0 to 1.5 grams/lb. This amount probably isn't necessary if you are eating enough total calories. Regular folks can get by with 0.4 to 0.5 grams per pound of bodyweight.

Do you need to take protein supplements?

Athletes do not have to rely on protein or amino acid supplements. There is no scientific evidence that protein or amino acids in supplements are more effective for athletes than protein in ordinary foods.

However, there is some evidence that some types of protein are used quicker and some slower. Whey protein is said to be absorbed faster. Casein (milk protein) is supposed to be slower in absorption so the benefits last over a period of time.

Another thing to consider is convenience. Protein supplements or meal replacement drinks are quick and easy to prepare. This is the best (and perhaps only) argument for taking protein supplements. Not a bad argument.

If you are looking for a cheaper version of a protein powder try nonfat dry milk. Not real tasty but it is inexpensive and will give you what you are looking for.

When should you eat protein?

At each meal! I could leave the answer at that; however, there is some evidence that meal timing can have a bearing on how well you fuel your body.

Eating foods or drinking liquids with small amounts of protein shortly before, and especially, after exercise is beneficial. Research shows that a little protein with carbohydrates stimulates recovery. Only small amounts of protein with carbohydrates are required for the positive effect after training. After a hard workout, you should have a recovery-rebuilding drink or snack. It should contain a small amount of protein with carbohydrates to repair and stimulate muscle proteins and to stock up muscle glycogen. Foods such as milk, yogurt, a sandwich, a protein-energy bar, or a nutrition shake or smoothie are all good choices.

Are all proteins alike?

In a word, no. Complete proteins contain all the essential amino acids your body needs. Proteins from animal sources (meat, eggs, milk, fish, etc.) tend to be complete proteins. Incomplete proteins lack one or more of the essential amino acids. These usually come from vegetables, grains, and nuts.

Vegetarian athletes need to be aware of this. For them to get all the essential amino acids needed, they must eat a variety of protein foods daily.

PE Protein Wrap

Eat a variety of proteins. Most people eat enough protein each day already; however, eating a variety of foods will ensure you get all the essential amino acids needed.

Pay attention to the protein you eat because some come with lots of unhealthy fat, like the juicy steak or whole milk. If you eat meat, eat lean cuts. Drink low fat or skim milk. For the vegetarian athlete, eat plenty of beans, soy, nuts, and whole grains to get all the essential amino acids. These offer protein (without much fat) and plenty of fiber.

> *"Red meat is not bad for you. Now, blue-green meat, that's bad for you!"*
> *—Tommy Smothers*

Reading the Labels

Reading package nutrition labels is not rocket science. It's spelled out pretty clear. Occasionally there could be some confusion but don't lose sleep over it. The "Nutrition Facts" label is required on most foods. It is a way to monitor what you are eating. It's an easy way to find out about serving sizes, fat content, cholesterol, sodium, carbohydrates and protein. The label is a quick way to help find out how much fat is in the product. The label spells out the total grams of fat, saturated fat, and cholesterol in each serving.

Generally this is what you'll find on the labels:

1. **Title:** "Nutrition Facts" this is the current nutritional information on the product in your hand.

2. **Serving Size:** Basic stuff here. It mentions how many servings are in the container. This can be confusing if you don't read it completely. If the serving size is one (as in one cookie) and you eat two, well simple math means you have to double the calories you're counting.

3. **Amount per serving:** This tells you how many calories are in each serving. Again sometimes confusing if you don't do the math. You may have a pack of cookies that says it has 4 servings if you eat the whole package you must multiply your calories by 4. You see how your calories can pile up.

4. **% Daily Value:** This is usually listed for a person that eats 2000 calories or 2500 calories. It's a percentage of what each serving brings to your diet.

5. **Total Fat:** This tells you how many calories are coming from fats.

6. **Saturated Fat:** One of the bad fats. It is listed under the total fats. This is one fat you want to keep low.

7. **Cholesterol:** Cholesterol has been linked to heart disease. Another thing to try to keep on the daily low side. The American Heart Association recommends less than 300 milligrams a day.

8. **Sodium:** Essentially salt. High salt intakes have been linked to high blood pressure. Normal people should try to stay around 2400 milligrams. Some athletes may need a little more during intense training.

9. **Total Carbohydrate:** This is where athletes get their energy. Athletes should be taking in about 60% carbs in their nutritional plan.

10. **Protein:** This is where you find out how many grams of protein you're getting in each serving. Athletes need only a little more than normal folks.

11. **Vitamins and Minerals:** This tells you the vitamin and mineral content of your food. If you aren't getting at least 100% you may need a supplement.

PE Label Wrap

Get comfortable with the nutrition labels. Having just a little more knowledge may give you an edge over your competition!

Another thing to locate on your food package is the expiration date. Sometimes it's around the nutrition label other times you'll have to search for it. This is very important if you happen to be taking supplements. I've actually seen out of date products on the shelves of health food store and drug stores.

"In general, mankind, since the improvement of cookery, eats twice as much as nature requires."
—Benjamin Franklin

Listen to Your Mother: Eat Your Fruits and Vegetables

"Nourish the mind like you would your body. The mind cannot survive on junk food."
—*Jim Rohn*

"Eat your fruits and vegetables!" I'm sure you've heard this from your parents or grandparents, or maybe even from the lunch lady. I know I did. But I didn't eat as many as I should have. You probably don't either. However, eating a lot of fruits and vegetables can help reduce your risk for heart disease and stroke; decrease high blood pressure and high cholesterol levels; help prevent some types of cancer; and can guard against cataracts and macular degeneration (common causes of vision loss).

So what's a lot? Well, more than you probably eat now. The latest dietary guidelines call for five to thirteen servings of fruits and vegetables a day. For a person who needs 2,000 calories a day to maintain weight and health, this means about 4½ cups per day.

Fruits, vegetables, and cardiovascular disease

There is some evidence that a diet filled with fruits and vegetables can lower the risk of heart disease.

Studies have found that the higher the average daily intake of fruits and vegetables, the lower the chances of developing heart disease. Those who averaged eight or more servings a day were 30% less likely to have a heart attack or stroke. (Get your parents and grandparents to read this!)

Increasing fruit and vegetable intake by as little as one serving per day can have an impact on reducing heart disease. In two Harvard studies, for every extra serving of fruits and vegetables added to a diet the chance of heart disease decreased by four percent.

Fruits and vegetables, blood pressure, and cholesterol

High blood pressure is a risk factor for heart disease and stroke. Diet can be a very effective tool for lowering blood pressure. A diet rich in fruits, vegetables, and low-fat dairy products and that restricts saturated and total fat will help reduce blood pressure.

Men and women with a high daily intake (more than four servings a day) have significantly lower levels of cholesterol than those who eat less fruits and veggies.

Fruits, vegetables, and cancer

There is limited evidence for a *cancer preventive* effect from eating fruit and vegetables for cancers of the mouth and esophagus, stomach, colon, larynx, lung, ovary (vegetables only), and bladder (fruit only).

Studies suggest that tomatoes can help protect men against prostate cancer. One of the pigments that give tomatoes their red color, lycopene, may be involved.

Fruits, vegetables, and vision

Eating a lot of fruits and vegetables can help keep your eyes in good condition. Fruits and vegetables can help prevent two age related eye disorders, cataracts and macular degeneration.

Cataract is the gradual clouding of the eye's lens. Macular degeneration, deterioration of the central portion of the retina, is the leading cause of blindness. Cataracts and macular degeneration starts as a blurred area in the center of your vision. As the disease spreads, your area of vision shrinks.

Dark green leafy vegetables contain the substances, lutein and zeaxanthin, which appear to help decrease potential harm to the eye. In general, a diet full of fruits and vegetables appears to reduce the chances of developing cataract or macular degeneration.

PE Mother Wrap

Eat your veggies and don't forget your fruit! Eat plenty and you can't go wrong.

"He that takes medicine and neglects diet wastes the skill of the physician."
—*Chinese Proverb*

Listen to Your Grandmother: Eat Your Fiber

What is it? Where is it? Carpet?

Fiber is considered a carbohydrate that can't be digested. Fiber is found in all the plants you eat. Not all fiber is the same. Soluble fiber dissolves incompletely in water. Insoluble fiber does not.

Current recommendations are that adults consume 20 to 40 grams of dietary fiber per day. Yet the average American eats only 12 to17 grams of dietary fiber a day.

Soluble Fiber Examples

Oat and Oat bran
Dried beans and peas
Barley
Flax seed (1/3 is soluble)
Fruits such as oranges and apples
Vegetables such as carrots

Insoluble Fiber Examples

Whole-wheat products
Wheat oat
Corn bran
Flax seed (2/3 is insoluble)
Vegetables such as green beans, cauliflowers and potato skins

Fruit skins and root vegetable skins

Health effects

Fiber can help reduce the risk of developing a variety of conditions; including heart disease, diabetes, diverticular (intestinal…guts) disease, and constipation. Studies are inconclusive regarding the effect of fiber in reducing colon cancer.

Heart disease

Heart disease is one of the leading causes of death in the U.S. This disease is described as a buildup of sludge (cholesterol-filled plaque) in the hearts' arteries. The buildup causes the arteries to become narrow and hard, creating a blockage and reducing blood flow, which can lead to a heart attack.

High intake of dietary fiber has been associated with a lower risk of heart disease. As much as a 40% lower risk of heart disease can be contributed to a diet high in fiber.

Type 2 diabetes

Type 2 diabetes is the most common form of diabetes. It is notorious for constant high blood sugar levels. The disease develops when the body can't produce enough insulin to keep blood sugar at normal levels. Sometimes the body pays no attention to the insulin that is produced. (www.diabetes.org)

There are several things that might help lower type 2 diabetes risk: keeping a healthy weight, being active, and not smoking. Studies have found that a diet high in cereal fiber is linked to a lower risk of type 2 diabetes.

Diverticular disease

Diverticulitis is an inflammation of the intestines (guts). In North America, it can affect one-third of people over age 45 and in two-thirds of people over age 85. That's not you—yet. And you don't want it to be. Some studies have found that diets high in dietary fiber have a link with reducing this disease by a whopping 40%.

Constipation

Constipation—stuffed up—not an appetizing subject. However it is the most common gut complaint in the U.S. The gastrointestinal tract (stomach and intestines) is responsive to fiber. Eating fiber foods reduces constipation. The fiber in wheat bran and oat bran seems to be particularly effective. If you run low in the fiber department, you should increase fiber intake gradually.

Tips for fiber intake

Eat more whole fruits instead of fruit juices. Substitute white rice, bread, and pasta with brown rice and whole-grain products. Choose whole-grain cereals for breakfast (eat some fruit with it). Snack on raw vegetables and fruit instead of chips and candy. Eat more nuts and seeds.

PE Grandmother Wrap

Eat your veggies, fruits, oats, and whole grains. This will allow you to "go" so that you can go on the field.

Putting It On or Taking It Off: Basics of Weight Gain and Weight Loss

Weight Gain

"I saw few die of hunger; of eating, a hundred thousand."
—*Benjamin Franklin*

Getting big and gaining weight tends to be what the majority of athletes (especially males) want the most. Girls are stuck in the middle. Girls may have the need or desire to gain weight for performance enhancement; however, they may be cautious because of society's perception in general. Girls have a much harder time with this topic than guys.

Gaining weight is the last thing that the majority of people sitting on the couch *watching* sports desire. Obviously, the key word here is watching. They are not performing. You are. That's only one of the things that separate you, the participant, from them, the spectators.

Will gaining weight help you in your sport? The short answers; it all depends on the sport, the position you play, and how much you weigh now. Putting on weight can provide an edge in sports that require power, leverage, and mass. Of course, you would rather have weight in the form of muscle rather than fat.

The basics

You may be reading this chapter first. If you are, this probably means you are in a sport that requires more size and strength.

Gaining weight is easy. It's just a matter of eating. I can hear some of you now, "But I do eat a lot. I eat like a horse." The problem is you eat like a small horse. Simple as that.

I could end this chapter here. But I won't. I realize that some people actually do have a hard time gaining weight. I was one of those people. I found however, gaining weight wasn't hard. Digging ditches—now that's hard. Gaining weight was unpleasant. Very unpleasant. It was unpleasant to eat as much as I did, but it was possible.

You need to have five things to be able to gain good weight...only five things.

1. Train hard

Be honest with yourself. That can be tough but try it anyway. Do you really train hard? Really, really hard? I'm sure some of you do. And I am equally sure some do not. Another couple of questions to ask yourself: do you train as hard as your competition? Do you train as hard as the hardest trainer on your team? If you ask most champions if they could have done anything else in their training they usually say yes. You see no matter what you achieve there is always something else you can do to improve.

By answering these questions truthfully you will find exactly where you fit under the category of *training hard.*

2. Good nutrition

No brainer here. Ask yourself some of the same questions. Do you really eat well? Really, really well? I'm sure some of you do. And I'm sure some don't. Another question to ask yourself; do you eat as well as your healthiest competitor? Or do you eat as well as the healthiest person on your team?

This is an area that most athletes neglect, especially compared to training. And it is the main reason you are reading this book!

3. Rest and recovery

Athletes often don't get enough rest. Some of this is because you are in school or studying for class (Am I dreaming here? Hope not.). Hey, school is important. It is much more important in life than anything you will do on the field. But that is a whole other topic.

An excuse used for not resting enough is hanging around with friends. There is nothing wrong with hanging out with friends, unless it cuts into your rest, training and nutrition.

Sleep is important. Sleeping well allows you to be physically and mentally rested for your next workout. You will not perform well if you are not able to focus on your sport. Often, athletes can get away with less sleep. Eventually, it will catch up with them. They'll have a bad game or practice, or worse, an injury. Just like you've always heard: try to get around seven or eight hours of sleep each night.

4. Desire

Desire is simply wanting something bad enough. Some people call this *will power*, while others call it *self-discipline*. Call it whatever you want. Basically, you have to want something bad enough to do all the things needed to achieve it.

You can't buy desire. You can't buy will power. You can't buy self-discipline. I looked and couldn't find them anywhere. What creates desire, will power, or self-discipline? The answer is simple. Desire, will power, and self-discipline are created by the *reasons* or *motives* behind your actions. In other words, if you have strong reasons you will succeed.

If you say to yourself, "I do want to gain weight. I just don't like to train." This is a poor excuse (See the *Excuses, Excuses, Excuses* chapter). The bottom line is you don't desire it bad enough to succeed. If you say to yourself, "I do want to gain weight. I just don't feel like eating like I should." This is another poor excuse. The bottom line is you don't have enough will power to succeed.

If you say to yourself, "I do want to gain weight, but I really like staying out late." What do we call this? Right, another pathetic excuse! The bottom line is (you guessed it) you don't have enough self-discipline to succeed.

Go back and work on your motives. They will drive you to having an increase in your desire.

5. Consistency

The last item you need and cannot do without is consistency and regularity. Which means, you must do all the above. You must be dedicated to yourself. No one can do this but you. If you don't do it, it won't get done. Nothing takes the place of being consistent with your desire, your nutrition, your training and your rest. Nothing.

There you have it. The mind controls the body. You are in control of your mind. Everything is a choice. The choices you make will follow you not only on the field, but also in life.

OK, I finished reading all that. So really, how do you gain weight?

After all this basic background stuff, I guess you want to know what to eat. Do I really have to write this all out? Probably, for some of you, but others have put the book down and are in the kitchen making something to eat. For those of you still here, read on.

Is it important for some athletes to gain weight?

Gaining weight is important for some sports. You definitely do not need a 250-pound cross-country runner. But a 250 pounder on a high school offensive line isn't a bad idea at all. Increases in weight are not necessarily muscle, but if you eat well and exercise correctly you'll have a better chance at gaining muscular tissue. The best time for gaining weight is during the off-season.

Does a healthy diet exist for an athlete?

Yes! You should follow a diet similar to one any healthy person would follow. Athletes just have to eat more. Eat a variety of foods. Be sure to eat regular meals and healthy snacks. These meals do not have to be huge. It is actually better for you to eat five to six small meals or snacks per day.

Fats, protein, and carbohydrates are all important (see the *Macs* chapter). On average your fat intake should be about 15 to 25%. Carbohydrate is the major source of energy your body uses during workouts. The amount that you need depends on your calorie needs, and the sport you play. In general, having 50 to 60% carbohydrates should work for most. Protein helps to build and repair muscle. Athletes need a little more than the average person. In general, protein should account for about 15 to 25% of your total calorie intake. Protein powder drinks or amino acid supplements are not necessary for weight gain if you follow a healthy and balanced diet. Occasionally, you may not have enough time to prepare meals. If time is short, then supplements are convenient and may be necessary.

Are certain foods more important to gain weight?

Experts in the field of sports nutrition report that total food intake is the most important. The nutrients considered most important for an athlete are carbohydrates. Yes, you read that correctly. Carbs!

A good weight-training program is necessary to stimulate muscle growth. It takes a lot of calories to do this type of training. A high-carbohydrate diet is necessary for maximum recovery of muscle energy (glycogen) your body stores. This will allow the muscles to work hard while training several days in a row.

So, how important is protein? Very important. You need protein to help build the muscle. But, if you don't have enough carbohydrates, your body will tend to use some of the protein for energy. You really don't want this to happen. You want the carbohydrates to fuel your workouts and you want the protein to rebuild your body. Carbohydrates are also considered protein sparing. So, in a sense they tend to preserve your muscles.

Essentially, weight-gain supplements by themselves will not build muscle and can be costly. A correct diet along with regular strength training will help you gain weight and build muscle.

Is there one fantastic exercise program for weight gain?

No. Not at all. There is not one great, fantastic program. There are so many different types of training programs it is easy to get confused. The old thoughts of high reps give you definition or cuts and low reps give you bulk just are not totally true.

Based on research, weight training can give you an increase in lean weight, bigger muscles and gains in strength. Gains in muscle size appear to be easier by multiple sets of 8 to 12 repetitions. Gains in strength and power come from using multiple sets with four to six repetitions.

Periodization is an approach to weight training that seems to produce superior gains in strength and power while possibly reducing potential injury. This type of workout involves moving from higher reps of 8 to 12 to lower reps of four to six over a period of months. Three days of working out (or more) per week are needed to get the most out of training. Periodically, multiple daily training sessions can also be used.

Endurance exercise by itself does not create lean body weight or strength and power. However, a combined aerobic and weight training program can increase endurance, lean muscle, and strength. On the other hand, if maximizing gains in muscle and strength are your main goals then aerobic training should be reduced or stopped all together. It really depends upon the demands of your sport.

Most successful programs will include overload, intensity, progression, and recovery. Recovery is a vital part of any program to be totally effective.

Timing

Research shows that eating within 15 to 30 minutes after a workout is the best time to start restoring protein and carbohydrate in the muscles. This will enhance recovery and help to prepare you for the next training session. Eating nutritiously during the next two to four hours after training can further improve recuperation and rebuilding.

A Simple Gaining Diet Plan

One way to figure out exactly where you are—from a calorie standpoint—is to write down everything you eat that has a calorie, liquid, or solid. Even semisolids like gum.

Just eat and train normally. During this time you aren't trying to gain or lose. You are just trying to maintain your normal body weight. Keep track of this for about a week. At the end of the week, total up your calories and divide the total by seven. The result is the number of how many calories it will take to maintain your present body weight.

All you have to do next is to add about 250 to 500 extra calories per day—preferably something nutritious. The calories must come from carbohydrates, protein, and fat. They are all important. If athletes don't eat enough calories, the body's protein is used for energy and potential muscle growth can be limited. Adding a small amount of calories like this will gradually increase your weight in a healthy manner.

If you don't want to keep track of the food intake for a week, you can try another formula, but it isn't as accurate. First, simply multiply your current weight by 10 and also 12 to get a range of what it takes to keep you where you are now. For example, if you weigh 175 pounds, you should multiply your weight by 10 and also 12. You'll get a range of 1750 to 2100 calories. You'll need around that amount of calories to keep your present bodyweight. To figure out what you need to gain weight, multiply your current weight by 15 and 16. The results will be (for a 175 pounder) between 2625 and 2800. This is the amount of calories you need to take in on a daily basis to gain weight.

What would be a healthy weight-gain goal?

This hasn't been studied as closely as losing weight. However, a healthy weight-gain goal should be about one quarter to one pound a week. Some people will actually gain more the first few weeks. Similar to people on weight loss diets who lose more the first few weeks. Gaining weight slowly allows you to avoid gaining too much body fat. The amount of weight you gain will depend on the amount of calories you eat. It also depends on your exercise program. Genetics will play a role. If you have skinny parents it may take more time, calories, and training to reach your goals.

How much muscle can you gain in a year?

This varies between athletes. Part of it has to do with genetics and part has to do with what you actually do in the weight room and the kitchen. These factors include: prior and proper weight training experience, present body weight, gender, diet, type of training program used, and motivation. It is very difficult, if not impossible, to just gain pure muscle. There will usually be some fat gain as well. If you plan your meals and seriously train, you should do well.

With males, 18 to 25 years old, it is possible to increase muscle mass as much as 20% during the first year of consistent weight training. This translates to possible gains of greater than 20 pounds a year, with approximately 18 pounds being lean body mass. This is not by training alone. If you don't feed the animal it will not grow. After a few years of regular training, mass gains may only be one to three percent per year.

Should emphasis be placed on dietary supplements compared to optimal resistance training and good overall nutrition?

Every so often, the "latest greatest supplement" is marketed that will produce quick and easy gains. Most of the time, it won't live up to the manufacturers claims. There is **no substitute** for participating in a good weight-training program, eating the right foods, and the right amount of food.

Dietary supplements should play a minor role in training. Way too much importance is placed on taking supplements. When athletes ask about supplements, most of the time their training programs are middle-of-the-road at best and they're probably not eating a good variety of food. The foundation of optimal performance is proper diet, training, and years of training in a particular sport.

Weight loss and performance

"I've been on a diet for two weeks and all I've lost is two weeks."
—Totie Fields

Coaches (and often teammates) make comments about weight and say your performance will improve if you lose a few pounds. Are they are right? What should you do? Think twice before you start skipping meals!

Is weight or fat loss beneficial?

Having lower body weight can reduce the amount of energy your body uses to perform. Consider how it feels to wear ankle weights or a weighted vest while training. Your body simply has to burn more energy to move your heavier body. Athletes with high percentages of body fat also have a harder time getting rid of body heat. Not good for the hefty football player during two-a-days in the hot, humid August heat.

In some activities (track, cheerleading, pole vaulting, high jump, swimming, high diving, gymnastics), it's almost impossible to have a lot of body fat and do well. In bodybuilding you aren't measured by your body fat percentage, but obviously, it can't be too high.

The minimum percentage of body fat considered safe for adults by the American College of Sports Medicine is 5% for males and 12% for females. Weight loss in teenagers should be done carefully, if at all. You do not want to jeopardize growth and development. And you could endanger yourself if you cut weight in an unhealthy way or by too much. The normal body fat average in adults is around 15% to 18% for men and 22% to 25% for women. Over 30% body fat can be considered overly fat or obese. The range for high-level athletes is lower than the average person. Keep in mind that body composition alone has *never* been a great predictor of sports performance.

Athletes often take low body fat too far. Girls can get into what is called the *female athlete triad*. The triad can occur when girls get caught up in performance or their physical looks and develop eating disorders, loss of periods, and bone loss (osteoporosis). Obviously their performance will suffer.

Losing weight rapidly will cause a drop in energy stores in the muscle and liver. A loss of fluid can also occur and will decrease athletic performance. Some athletes, especially those who compete in weight classes such as boxers, wrestlers, weight lifters and martial arts, sometimes follow "starvation" diets. Following this type of diet, the athlete may give up food almost entirely. It is not uncommon for this to occur for a couple of days to a whole week. Weight will drop. Performance levels can drop as well. Long-term calorie reduction can also reduce the supply of needed vitamins and minerals.

So, too little body fat can create some pretty bad consequences. And too much body fat can be pretty bad as well. Men with over 25% body fat and women with over 32% body fat can begin to have many other problems. These include type 2 diabetes, high blood pressure, stroke, heart disease, and certain cancers. When the bulk of the fat is located around the belly, the risks are even greater.

Fat. What's it good for?

Fat is vital to ensure the proper functioning of the body. Fats supply the *essential* fatty acids, which are not made by the body. These essentials must be taken in from food. Linoleic acid is the most important essential fatty acid (particularly for the growth of babies).

The body's spare calories are fats and are an important energy source. In general, the body tends to use carbohydrates for energy first then it turns to fats. Fat also helps to protect the body by providing cushioning for the internal organs and bones.

It's my parents' fault.

Come on now. Not everything can be blamed on your parents. There is some genetic control over your weight. Not everyone can be perfect...whatever that is. However, genetics aside, you can still make a great deal of difference with proper training and diet. Some people are lucky to have two genetically perfect parents. I've never met that person.

When should you lose weight?

Athletes should consider weight loss during the off-season. This will avoid potentially harmful or performance decreasing effects of dieting during the in-season.

How much loss is safe?

In general losing one to two pounds per week is considered safe. This amount of weight loss is gradual and less stressful to your body. Often, there is more weight lost in the first week but it tends to level out.

Are there supplements to lose weight?

There are. Some work and some don't. In general, they are not recommended for use. If you are a young athlete, you don't need a short cut because of the possible hazards to your body and the possibility of hurting your performance.

A magic pill does not exist that will speed up fat loss. Be careful of the claims you see at the health food stores or in magazines. The testimonials made for the "magical" benefits may not be true. The Dietary Supplement and Health Education Act (DSHEA) passed by Congress in 1994 allow unproven and understudied supplements to be sold. These supplements may not be held to any high standards. The scariest thing is that there is no guarantee that the product label is true.

The basics

Losing weight can be easy. It's only a matter of not eating as much as you would like! End of chapter! Just kidding. I realize that some people actually do have a difficult time losing weight. Losing weight isn't hard. At least not as hard as two-a-days in August. Weight loss is very unpleasant. The basics for weight loss ring true as they do for weight gain. You have five rules to be able to lose weight.

1. Train hard

Honesty is the best policy and now you have to be honest with yourself. Do you train hard enough? Some of you do and of course some of you don't. How about the people around you? Do you train as hard as the toughest person on your team? How about your competition? Do you think you train as hard as they do? Answer these questions with honesty and you'll know where you stand.

If you ask most champions, "Is there anything else you could have done in your training?" They will usually say, "Yes!" Then proceed to give you a list of things. This is true whether they are winning or losing. No matter high up on the ladder you are you can always do a bit more.

2. Good nutrition

Ask yourself some of the same questions you did above. Do you really eat well? Some do and most don't. Do you eat as well as your healthiest competitor? Or do you eat as well as the healthiest person on your team? Do you eat too much? Do you eat the right amount of the right foods? Do you eat at the right times? This is a major area that athletes neglect. You are on the road to better nutrition by reading this book.

3. Rest and recovery

Athletes don't always get enough rest. It could be because you're in school or studying (am I hallucinating here?). School is essential. Don't neglect your studies. It is much more important in life than anything you will do on the field. But that's another topic.

People have many excuses for what they do or don't do (see the *Excuses* chapter). An excuse commonly used is hanging around with friends. Hanging out with friends is great! But don't let it cut into your studies, rest, training or meals.

A good night's sleep prepares you physically and mentally for your next workout. Some people may get away with less sleep, but eventually it catches up with them. A bad performance or practice or even injury occurs. You've heard it before: get around seven or eight hours of sleep each night.

4. Desire

Desire is simply wanting something bad enough. Some people call this *will power* and others call it *self-discipline*. What you call it doesn't matter. What it boils down to is you have to want something so much you'll do all the right things to get it.

Desire, will power, self-discipline cannot be bought. I looked and couldn't find them anywhere. What creates desire, will power, and self-discipline? Simple, it's the reasons behind your actions. Look for good reasons. Find good reasons. If the reasons are strong enough you will succeed.

If you say to yourself, "I do want to lose weight. I just don't like to train." or "I do want to lose weight. I just don't feel like eating like I should." or "I do want to lose weight but I really like staying out late." All feeble excuses. The bottom line (you guessed it); you don't have enough desire, will power or self-discipline to succeed. This also means that your reasons are not strong enough.

5. Consistency

The last item you need and cannot do without is consistency. Which means you must work at the previous four areas constantly and consistently. Be dedicated to yourself. No one can do this for you. If you don't do it, it won't get done. Nothing takes the place of being consistent with desire, nutrition, training and rest. Nothing.

The mind controls the body. Believe it or not you are in control of your mind.

It is all a choice. The choices you make will follow you on the field and in life. Choose success.

A Simple Reducing Diet Plan

A simple way to figure out exactly where you are from a calorie standpoint is to write down everything you eat that has a calorie, or is a liquid or solid. Even Jell-O.

Just eat and train like you usually do. During this time you aren't trying to gain or lose. You are just trying to maintain your normal body weight. Keep track of your food intake for about a week. At the end of the week add up your calories. Then divide by seven. The number you get is approximately the number of calories it will take to maintain your present body weight.

All you have to do next is to subtract about 250 to 500 calories per day—preferably fat calories. Following a simple plan like this should result in steady weight loss of around one to two pounds a week.

PE Weight Wrap

Weight loss without an undesirable effect on performance is only possible if the loss is planned ahead. This should happen over an adequate and safe time period. A sufficient supply of carbohydrates, proteins, vitamins, minerals, and water is absolutely necessary for the health of the athlete.

"Life asks us to make measurable progress in a reasonable time. That's why they make those fourth grade chairs so small."
—*Jim Rohn*

The Simple Chapter: Simple Bulking Tips and Simple Burning Tips

"What you have to do and the way you have to do it are incredibly simple. Whether you are willing to do it, that's another matter."
—Peter F. Drucker

Simple Bulking Tips

You need to realize the only way to bulk up is to take in more calories during the day than you burn off! If you fail at this you won't reach your goal. So, you have three choices. You can either raise your calories, change your training, or a combination of the two. You don't want to raise your calories too rapidly or you'll gain more fat than muscle. Start by increasing your daily calories by 250 calories and not more than 500. If you level off after a few weeks add another 200 to 250 calories at that time.

Calorie cycling

This has nothing to do with eating on a bicycle. Calorie cycling is a term used for fluctuating your daily calories over the course of a week. Say your average daily calorie intake is 3500 calories. If you want to gain some weight you add 250 calories more per day. Instead of maintaining exactly 3750 calories a day you try to hit that number as an average over the course of a week. Some days you may eat 3500 calories and the next 3800 followed by 3700 and so on. Think of this as being similar to changing your workouts between heavy, medium, and lighter weights. Or for runners, this is similar to fluctuating your training. Some days running intervals, other days an easy medium-length run, or another day of hills.

Meals

Obviously, your meals are important not only to lose weight but to gain weight as well. Throughout the day, you should have several smaller meals instead of three big ones. If you need 3500 calories a day just try to divide your total calories over the course of the day.

1. **Always eat breakfast.** Your body has been doing without food for about six to ten hours. It needs food. Try to eat a breakfast that includes protein and complex carbohydrates. To be a real fanatic about this, you could limit your carbohydrates at breakfast to the lower glycemic index (see the *Macs* chapter).

2. **Meal 2 or Snack 1.** You can eat real food like fruit, veggies and a protein source (meat, fish, etc). Eating a snack or meal like this would be great but you are still in school! So it will be more convenient for you to have a meal replacement bar or a canned shake. They are quick and easy. I wish I could say they tasted good but the taste is adequate at best. However, you aren't eating for taste, you are fueling your body for performance!

3. **Meal 3, Snack 2**, Lunch, call it "Fred" if you want to but eat something nutritious.

4. **Pre workout.** About an hour or two before your workout eat a small 200 to 300 calorie snack. This should be low in fat and fiber so you reduce the chances of feeling bloated.

5. **Post workout.** Here, timing is important. Your body is craving food to replenish what the fuel it has used. This is also where recuperation begins. A meal as described in number 2 would be fine; however, you really want to get something in your stomach within 15 to 30 minutes after the workout. Simple carbohydrates at this time are fine. The easiest type of meal is a liquid one containing carbohydrates and protein. The protein source doesn't matter; however there is evidence that a whey protein is absorbed more quickly however there is research that also finds that at this time just getting some type of protein is better than none.

6. **Supper, dinner, or Meal 6.** Eat your regular meal. Complex carbohydrates are the carbs of choice at this time.

7. This is an **optional snack**. It may seem like you are eating all the time but it's just part of the drill. This optional meal is obviously between supper and bedtime. If you have a snack at this time, have some protein food and try to limit carbohydrate calories to lower glycemic carbohydrates.

To summarize all this stuff. There are actually two most important meals: breakfast and the after-workout snack. But don't skip any of the meals. Have several meals and snacks during the day. Complex carbohydrates (and low glycemic) are the carbs of choice except after your workout. Calorie cycling breaks up the process and some bodies respond well to this technique. Change happens over time, not over night.

Supplements

If you follow a good plan, supplements are not necessary. However, supplements are great for your snack meals ("Fred") and post workout meal. Taking a multivitamin mineral tablet would be fine. See the *Sports Supplement* chapter for more information. If you wished to try an inexpensive milk protein supplement, try nonfat dry milk.

Cardio

Cardio is an important part of conditioning. The amount of cardio you do depends entirely upon your sport. A cross-country runner is going to do more cardio than the offensive lineman. If you are trying to put on a few pounds you may wish to decrease some of the cardio you are doing.

> *"I have the simplest tastes. I am always satisfied with the best"*
> —Oscar Wilde

Simple Fat Burning Tips

You need to realize that the only way to lose fat is to burn more calories during the day then you take in! Fail at this you won't reach your goal. You have three choices. Lower your calories, increase your training, or a combination of the two. Don't reduce your calories to fast because your body will try to compensate. Start by reducing your daily calories by 250 calories and not more than 500. If you level off after a few weeks, drop another 200 to 250 calories at that time. Never starve yourself because your body and performance will suffer.

Calorie cycling

Calorie cycling is a term used for an idea of varying your daily calories during the week. For example, your average daily calorie intake is 3500 calories. If you want to lose some fat, you cut it by 250. Instead of maintaining exactly 3250 calories a day you try to hit that number as an average over the course of a week. So some days you may eat 3000 calories and the next 3300 followed by 3200 and so on. Think of this as being similar to changing your workouts between heavy, medium, and lighter weights.

Meals

Obviously your meals are important. Decreasing bodyweight can actually follow a similar plan as gaining only you will cycle downward. You should have several smaller meals (instead of three big ones) throughout the day. If you need 3200 calories a day, divide your total calories over the course of the day.

1. **Always eat breakfast.** Your body has been fasting for about six to ten hours. It needs food. Eat a breakfast that includes protein and complex carbohydrates. For the real fanatic: limit your carbohydrates at breakfast to the lower your glycemic ones (see the *Macs* chapter).

2. **Meal 2 or Snack 1.** Eat real food like fruit, veggies and some protein (meat, fish, etc). While eating like this is great it may be difficult since you are in school. It's probably more convenient for you to have a meal replacement bar or canned shake because they are quick and easy. They may not taste great but remember you aren't eating for taste right now. You're fueling for performance!

3. **Meal 3, Snack 2.** Lunch! Eat something nutritious! While some school lunchrooms may not have executive chefs preparing the meals the food should suffice.

4. **Pre workout.** Don't eat anything that is full of fiber or fat. You might feel too full to perform well. About an hour or two before your workout have a small 200 to 250 calorie snack.

5. **After training.** Timing is important. Your body is craving nutrients to stock up what it has used. This is where recuperation and recovery actually begins. A meal as described in number 2 would be fine. The key is you want to get something in your stomach within 15 to 30 minutes after the workout. Simple carbohydrates at this time are fine. The easiest type of meal is a liquid containing carbohydrates and protein.

6. **Supper, dinner, or Meal 6.** Eat your regular meal. Complex carbohydrates are the carbs of choice at this time.

To summarize all these bits and pieces. There are actually two most important meals: breakfast and the after-workout snack. Don't skip meals and have several during the day. Complex carbohydrates (and low glycemic) are the carbohydrates of choice except after your workout. Calorie cycling breaks up the process and some bodies respond well to this technique. Don't drop your calories too fast.

Drinks

Reduce or eliminate sugary soda drinks. If you drink them, drink the diet versions. To some of you, the diet versions may not taste good. So what? If you really think about it this type of drink isn't necessary. These drinks won't get you any closer to your athletic goals. They add a bunch of unnecessary calories.

There has been some debate about diet drinks that are sweetened with aspartame. Some studies have found there may be health risks however others have not. At this time is it legal and the FDA says it is safe. A few years ago there was a cancer scare about the use of saccharin. Anything that had saccharin in it had to have a label similar to the ones on tobacco.

So if you truly wanted to cut calories leave off the regular versions. If you have an aversion or an allergy to the artificial sweeteners in the drinks stay away from them as well. Again neither is necessary for athletic enhancement.

Alcohol. You are too young to be drinking legally. What's more alcohol won't get you any closer to your athletic goals. Remember, whatever doesn't get you closer to your goals actually takes you farther away from them.

Supplements

Supplements aren't necessary if you plan your meals well. Of course that is sometimes a huge task. Taking a multivitamin mineral tablet is fine just in case you are not getting enough nutrients through a normal diet.

There is no need at all for any high school athlete to take any fat burner supplement. According to the FDA they won't make much of a difference. And just about all of them say that for them to work you need to be exercising. Duh! Follow a plan of exercise, eat what you are supposed to and you'll have no problems.

Cardio

No magic here. Again, cardio work of some type will allow you to burn off more calories. There is some evidence that the time you do cardio can have an effect on how many calories you burn. When you get up in the morning your levels of stored carbohydrate is low. That is because of the amount of time between your last meal and when you woke up. Say after practice you had dinner around 7:30 pm and you usually have breakfast (you'd better be eating breakfast!) around 7:00 am. That's over 11 hours without food! During this time of watching TV, talking on the phone, playing video games, sleeping, and maybe even studying, your stored carbohydrates (glycogen) are being slowly being used. They aren't being used up as much as a training session, but they are being used. When you wake up in the morning your energy stores are a bit depleted. It has been speculated that this low glycogen and blood sugar time period is the best time to burn fat because your primary fuel source has already decreased. It has also been suggested that after exercising in the morning there can be an after burn effect. Essentially, this means that extra calories can be used the first few hours after exercise.

If you can't do the cardio in the morning then the next best time to do it is after weight training. Weight training uses carbohydrates as its primary fuel source. So, if that source is depleted, your body should lean on your fat stores a bit more.

PE Simple Wrap

Life is simple. Do the right things and great things follow. Gaining or losing weight can be simple as well.

> *Don't dig your grave with your own knife and fork.*
> *—English Proverb*

Filling The Gas Tank: Fluid Replacement

"The best and fastest way to learn a sport is to watch and imitate a champion."
—Jean-Claude Killy

Your body is made up of roughly 60 to 70% water. On a normal day, you could lose about six glasses of water through pee (urine) and another three to four glasses just from sweating and breathing. So besides losing fluid during training you can lose a significant amount of fluid just sitting around in an air-conditioned room.

Drinking water is a good choice for maintaining fluid. You can also get water from juice, milk, coffee, tea, soda, fruits, and vegetables.

Basically, the average person needs eight to nine glasses per day just to replace normal losses. You aren't normal or average. You are an athlete. Athletes can lose about five times as much fluid as a couch potato.

Dehydration

You begin to get dehydrated after only a two percent water loss. Your performance will also drop off. Dehydration can affect your performance in less than an hour of training. This can happen even sooner, if you start the session already dehydrated. And this is only with a two percent loss. It doesn't take much to lose two percent. This can happen on the field or even if you are sick in bed with the flu.

Early symptoms of dehydration are headaches, dry eyes, drowsiness, loss of concentration, and irritability. Muscle cramps are also a sign of poor fluid replacement and loss of electrolytes. Thicker blood, faster heart rate, and blood pressure changes are other symptoms. Dehydration of more than three percent of your weight increases the risk of heat illness, heat cramps, heat exhaustion, and heat stroke.

Essentially, your brain won't work right, you'll feel slow, and out of it. Your kidneys won't function correctly causing a build up of wastes. You'll have trouble regulating your body temperature, especially during hot and humid days. You'll feel overheated. Some athletes get constipated. Yep, stuffed up.

Dehydration during exercise can lead to poor heat loss. This can raise the body's core temperature. The temperature rise can cause a strain on the cardio-vascular system. Often, athletes with high-body fat can get dehydrated faster than athletes with low-body fat under the same weather conditions. Some studies have shown that re-hydration can take 24 hours or more. If you are training to increase your performance, this is not a state to get into.

What should you drink?

If you exercise for an hour or less, drinking water should be fine. However, if you are training over an hour, sports drinks will replace your fluid and provide energy as well. Sports drinks also can replace lost electrolytes. In general, sports drinks should contain six to eight percent carbohydrate concentration (60 to 80 calories and 12 to 15 carbohydrates per eight ounces). Studies have found no improvement in performance or hydration with drinks loaded with over eight percent carbohydrates. Cool drinks are absorbed better than room temperature or warm beverages.

Is there anything you shouldn't drink for re-hydration?

Skip any drinks over eight percent carbohydrates. This includes any fruit juices or sodas. Drinks with caffeine or alcohol shouldn't be used because of the possible risk of dehydration that can come with excess urine production. This also includes those highly marketed "energy" drinks laced with large amounts of caffeine and sugar.

When and how much should you drink?

You probably drink when you're thirsty right? Unfortunately, by the time you get thirsty, you can be on the road to dehydration. To avoid dehydration, drink fluids before, during, and after exercise.

During your normal days drink around 8 to 12 cups of water a day. Ideally, you will want to weigh yourself before you train. A couple of hours before exercise you may want to drink one or two cups of a sports drink. Some research shows, drinking a sports drink with a bit of protein can be beneficial toward recovery. About 10 to 15 minutes before training drink a cup of water. During exercise, take water breaks approximately every 15 to 20 minutes. Weigh yourself after exercise and then drink about two cups of fluid for every pound of body weight you lost.

Is there a difference between water and sports drinks?

Yes. In general, water is good for exercise that lasts under an hour. However, this is also dependant on the conditioning of the athlete, body fat percentage of the athlete, and how hot it is outside. If the athlete is a heavy sweater, water may not help as much as a sports drink. For some athletes, a sports drink can be necessary during this time.

For longer periods of training or training in intense heat, sports drinks are much better than water. They provide carbohydrate for energy and help with recuperation. They provide electrolytes, such as sodium and potassium. The sodium helps in re-hydration as athletes need more sodium than the average human. Sports drinks are absorbed quicker than water. They can delay exhaustion during training. Sports drinks during training can allow you to workout longer and harder and they taste better, too.

How do you tell if you are dehydrated?

Good question! You should weigh before and after practice. Generally, for every pound lost during training you should drink about 16–20 ounces of fluid. If this fluid isn't replenished, the player risks dehydration during the next training session.

You can also check the color of your pee (urine). If it kinda looks like apple juice (a dark, gold color) you may already be a little dehydrated. If it looks pale like lemonade then you're on the re-hydration highway.

PE Fluid Wrap

Drink throughout the day. There is no excuse for dehydration.

"Doctors and scientists said that breaking the four-minute mile was impossible, that one would die in the attempt. Thus, when I got up from the track after collapsing at the finish line, I figured I was dead."
—*Roger Bannister (After becoming the first person to run a four-minute mile, 1954)*

The BAD Stuff: Tobacco, Alcohol, Steroids

"To be prepared is half the victory."
—*Miguel de Cervantes; Spanish Novelist, Poet, Playwright*

Tobacco

So what does tobacco use have to do with nutrition? Read on. So you thought tobacco could only cause cancer or lung problems down the line? Read on. Think you could quit before any real bad effects happened to you? Read on!

Smoking helps kill more people than AIDS, alcohol, drugs, car crashes, murders, suicides, and fires all together. Tobacco use can be the single most preventable cause of all deaths in the U.S. This is because smoking is a choice. No one forces you to smoke.

About two-thirds of all teenagers try smoking. Around half that number will become regular daily smokers. Eighty-five percent of smokers start before they are 16 years old. Most current smokers think they could quit anytime. Actually, *only three percent* of all people who try to quit smoking each year will succeed.

Research has shown that athletes who play at least one sport are 40% less likely to be smokers. The more sports you play, the less likely you are to smoke. So one good thing about being an athlete is you are less likely to smoke.

Vitamins and tobacco

Smoking can use up many essential vitamins and minerals. It can also affect the way the body can use these nutrients. For example, vitamin C is lost every time you smoke. There is also evidence that vitamin E is affected. Since you damage yourself every time you light up you need more and more vitamins to try and decrease the damage you inflict upon yourself. Don't kid yourself here. Vitamins will not stop all the damage of smoking.

What is in the smoke?

Cigarette smoke has around 4,000 materials. This includes around 200 poisons such as benzene, formaldehyde, carbon monoxide, ammonia, propane, and cyanide. The make up of the smoke depends on the tobacco and how it's packed, the length of the cigarette (or cigar), the type of filter and paper, and the tobacco temperature while smoking. The drug nicotine is in cigarettes and tar is a by-product.

What are the side effects?

Some of the stuff in tobacco will slow down protective movement in the lungs. There is evidence that tobacco can be cancerous. Even smokeless tobacco may cause lip or mouth cancer. Some by products of smoking may also have a role in bladder cancer. A pinch of smokeless can have the same effects as smoking three or four cigarettes. So far none of this enhances sports performance!

Nicotine is a very addictive drug. It can increase the heart rate and can raise blood pressure. It can also increase breathing, lower HDL levels (the good fats), and tighten blood vessels. Nicotine can increase oxygen requirements of the heart muscle, but also can lower oxygen supply. In some people it can also deaden the taste buds.

The use of nicotine in high doses is deadly. Nicotine poisoning depends on the dose. Small doses can cause nausea and vomiting, dizziness, headache, diarrhea, increased heart rate, blood pressure elevation, and sweating. People generally recover. Larger doses can create mouth, throat and stomach burning sensations as well as any of the other listed symptoms. This can progress to convulsions, irregular heart rates, respiratory failure caused by muscle paralysis, and coma. Death can occur within minutes to hours.

If smoking doesn't get you sooner, it will get you later. It has been estimated that every time you light up it takes about 5 to 20 minutes off your life.

Other problems associated with smoking

Recent research found that the risk of developing rheumatoid arthritis was nearly double for current smokers compared to non-smokers. Rheumatoid arthritis is an autoimmune disease. Basically, your body attacks itself. It causes inflammation of the joints, the tissue around the joints, and sometimes other body organs.

A number of studies suggest that smokers have a three to four times higher risk for developing degenerative disc disease (DDD). A disc is a cushion found between the vertebrae of the spinal column. Smoking can also aggravate pre-existing disc degeneration.

Interestingly enough, smokers can also have an increased risk (53%) of divorce. A study of 33, 000 adults found that smoking rates were above average among men and women who later divorce. Evidently, smoking may be a predictor of divorce and apparently age, race, education, income, or gender makes no difference. This does not mean smoking will cause a divorce. It means those who smoke have characteristics and experiences which can make them more likely to divorce than nonsmokers.

Smoking can increase the development of wrinkles and yellow teeth. Lower bone density has been found. This increases the risk of bone loss or osteoporosis. It can also cause fertility problems in both men and women. Smoking has also been found to decrease sexual health in males.

Smokers tend to get more colds, flu, bronchitis, and pneumonia than non-smokers. People with certain health conditions, like asthma, become sicker if they smoke or if they're around people who smoke.

Smoking can affect the body's ability to repair itself. Common sports injuries such as damage to tendons and ligaments will heal more slowly in smokers than nonsmokers. Rotator cuff tears in smokers can be twice as large as those in non-smokers. Healing after surgery is also slower in smokers.

One study found children and teenagers exposed to tobacco smoke, even at extremely low levels, is linked to decreases in certain skills, including reading, math, and logic and reasoning.

Bad breath and bad smelling clothes, skin, and hair are common. Smoking and vitamin deficiencies have also been linked to premature graying.

So how does this affect sport performance?

Smoking has a damaging effect on performance. Smoking can weaken lung function so there is less oxygen available for muscles during training. Smokers tend to suffer from shortness of breath almost three times more often than nonsmokers. Most smokers can't run or walk as fast or as far as nonsmokers. Smoking also increases fatigue during and after exercise. Smokers get less benefit from physical training, have less muscular strength and flexibility, and experience disturbed sleep patterns compared to nonsmokers.

Is there any other down side?

How about expense? Smoking can be expensive. Depending on where you live and the brand you smoke, a pack of cigarettes a day can cost around $1500 to $2000 dollars a year. That's money you could spend on CDs, video games, dates, or even on supplements.

Alcohol

> *"Beer is proof that God loves us and wants us to prosper."*
> —Benjamin Franklin

What was good for Benjamin Franklin is definitely not good for athletes. In the past it was thought that alcohol could improve performance. Long distance runners were given brandy. Bodybuilders would drink some wine before going on stage. Some athletes believe a small amount of alcohol will enhance performance by decreasing nervous tension and increasing self-confidence. They are wrong.

Does alcohol enhance athletic performance?

No. As a matter of fact alcohol reduces performance. Alcohol is a depressant. It slows the breathing rate. Exactly the opposite effect athletes need. Drinking alcohol can decrease reaction time, balance, accuracy, hand to eye coordination, strength, power, speed, muscle endurance, and overall endurance. Not exactly a performance enhancing drug. During recovery, alcohol interferes with the loading of carbohydrates in muscles for later use. Alcohol can also lengthen the recovery times from an injury.

In the past people thought athletes could replace carbohydrate stores by drinking beer. Waste of time! Most regular 12-ounce beers provide about 16 grams of carbohydrate. Even less for light beers. This isn't very much. Not enough for loading carbohydrates or for recovery. Most sports drinks have more and are obviously better for you.

Alcohol stimulates the kidneys to make urine. Yep, it makes you go to the bathroom. It is a diuretic and can make your body lose water and possibly become dehydrated. Dehydration has a negative effect on performance (see the *Filling Your Tank* chapter). You need to be well hydrated in most sports, especially endurance sports and sports like basketball and football. Dehydration increases the risk of heat stroke or heat exhaustion during exercise. About four ounces of body fluid are lost for each drink of alcohol. Water loss caused by drinking booze will cause the additional loss of minerals such as magnesium, potassium, calcium, and zinc. These are vital to keeping the fluid balance and for nerve and muscle action.

Alcohol's undesirable effects hang around long afterwards. Why do you think they call it a hang over? Reaction time, balance, strength, power, and quickness all suffer the morning after.

Going over to the dark side:

- More than 100,000 deaths are caused by alcohol consumption each year in the U.S. Direct and indirect causes of death include driving, liver disease, falls, cancer, and stroke.

- Sixty-five percent of youth say they got the alcohol from family or friends.

- Kids who drink alcohol are 50 times more likely to use cocaine than those who never drink.

- Males are four times as likely as females to be heavy drinkers.

- Underage drinking costs the U.S. more than $58 billion every year.

- Alcohol is the most commonly used drug among young people.

- People with drinking problems average four times as many days in the hospital as nondrinkers.

- Alcohol kills 6½ times more youth than all other illicit drugs combined.

- About 18 million Americans meet the criteria for alcoholism

- Alcohol plays a role in one in four cases of violent crime

- More than 16,000 people die each year in automobile accidents in which alcohol was involved

If you don't drink, there is no good reason to start.

Anabolic Steroids

I hope you folks didn't come to this chapter first! If you did...read the following very carefully. Drug use is serious, can be illegal, and nothing to play around with.

What are anabolic steroids?

Anabolic steroids are man-made versions similar to the male sex hormone testosterone. They can be injected or taken as pills. There has been some use through the skin (transdermally) but this is not common in athletics. In general the pill form can create more of the side effects, especially in the liver. Anabolic steroids are useful in enhancing athletic performance. However the undesirable side effects can harm your health permanently.

Steroids are a controlled substance. This means you must have a doctor's prescription to legally use them. It is against the law to have or deal anabolic steroids for non-medical uses. Steroids do have acceptable medical uses. They can be used to treat or improve weight loss due to severe illness or surgery, infection, to control breast cancer in women, to treat osteoporosis (bone loss), certain kinds of anemia, burns, or when males produce unusually low amounts of testosterone. The doses used to treat these medical conditions are much lower than the typical doses used in sports.

Another type of steroid, corticosteroids, are used to reduce inflammation and swelling. They are also used to treat certain skin conditions and asthma. This drug is necessary in some injuries or disease processes. Corticosteroids are not anabolic steroids. However, like all medications they do have some side effects such as: increased appetite, deposits of fat in chest, face, upper back, and stomach, water retention leading to swelling, high blood pressure, diabetes, black and blue marks, slowed wound healing, osteoporosis, cataracts, acne, muscle weakness, thinning of the skin, stomach ulcers, increased sweating, mood swings, and depression.

Anabolic steroids have two general effects: *anabolic and androgenic.*

Anabolic

Typically this is what athletes want. Anabolic steroids are shown to increase fat-free weight gain and muscle if used with a strength-training program. Good nutrition is also necessary to get the full benefit. Strength gains commonly occur.

It is not known if the gains are from using the drug, having harder workouts, or being able to recover faster from the workouts. Taking steroids and not working out will not change your body.

Androgenic

These are the effects you don't want, especially girls. These are the secondary male features such as: an Adam's apple, deeper voice, acne and rougher skin texture, larger hands and feet, broader shoulders and chest, heavier bone structure, increased muscle mass, physical strength, and abdominal, facial, chest and pubic hair.

Major side effects

There are side effects to every medicine you take. This is true whether you need a doctor's prescription or buy them over the counter. Some of the side effects will go away when you stop using the steroids and some may not. You could get some of the side effects, none of the side effects, or all of the side effects. You just don't know which it will be. That is until you take them and then it could be too late.

Liver damage

Most of the steroids taken by mouth can cause abnormal liver function. These abnormalities range from the common, but usually harmless, increase of liver enzymes to rare, but very serious, tumors and bleeding. The majority of the serious side effects come from oral steroids.

The increase of liver enzymes usually stops gradually when athletes discontinue using the steroids. It has been noted however, that liver enzymes can register in the high normal ranges with intense exercise.

Heart disease

Some athletes who use anabolic steroids can develop high blood pressure. It appears that the increase in blood pressure is dose dependent. The more steroids you take the higher the blood pressure can get. After stopping steroid use the blood pressure usually (key word: *usually*) gets back to normal in about six to eight weeks.

Athletes can also have decreased amounts of the good cholesterol. The combination of high blood pressure and low HDL-cholesterol can increase the chance of getting heart disease at an earlier age.

Sex and reproduction

Taking large amounts of anabolic steroids can shrink testicles (nads, balls, nuts, nards, family jewels, goodies, cojones, eggs, Rocky Mountain Oysters, gonads, twig and berries, bits and pieces, frank and beans, skin chandelier, or what ever you want call them). What ever you call them you don't want them to shrink. These athletes can also have poor sperm production and some can become functionally sterile. This means, they produce sperm but do not produce good quality sperm. Sperm count and testicle size may not return to normal for several months after stopping the steroids.

Steroid use can lead to *gynecomastia*. The term comes from the Greek words for women-like breasts. Most males probably don't want this to happen. It is a common problem that occurs naturally but there is an increased risk by taking anabolic steroids. Gynecomastia regularly affects about 40 to 60% of men. It can affect one side of the chest or both. Although steroids are linked with male boobs, there is no definitive cause in the majority of cases. In most women the opposite is true. Steroid use may cause breast shrinkage.

Other male effects of steroid use experienced by females include increased facial hair, male patterned baldness, and a deeper voice. Additional possible effects are irregularity or absence of the menstrual cycle (which can also happen with low body fat percentages), clitoris enlargement, and shrinking of the uterus. Baldness, facial hair, enlargement of the clitoris, and deepening of the voice are usually *irreversible*. Doesn't make for an attractive girl.

Psychological

Common psychological side effects include increases (and sometimes decreases) in sex drive, aggressive behavior, a "feeling of well being", depression, sleeping disorders, anxiety, and psychological addiction to the drugs.

"Roid rage" is something that has been in the news frequently. While the drugs don't necessarily turn people into monsters, they can amplify tendencies people already have. This means, if you are already naturally aggressive you can run the risk of being even more aggressive and violent. Not good.

Growth

Normal growth usually begins to stop after sexual maturation; however some people up to 18 years and over may still be growing. If younger athletes abuse steroids, the growth plates of the long bones can close earlier than usual. The person can end up being a bit shorter as a result of using the steroids.

Skin

Possible rougher skin and increased acne. Who wants this? As if things weren't bad enough.

PE Bad Wrap

In the long run, taking steroids is not worth it.

"The winners in life think constantly in terms of I can, I will, and I am. Losers, on the other hand, concentrate their waking thoughts on what they should have or would have done, or what they can't do."
—*Dennis Waitley*

Myths, Legends and Lies in Nutrition

"Everybody's a self-made man. Only the successful ones are ever willing to admit it."
—*Anonymous*

Everyone is looking for the secret—the little pill, powder, drink, or workout—to give him or her an edge over the competition. There is a great deal of poor information out there. The following are a few of the most common myths, misconceptions, and outright lies.

Carbohydrates and sugar should be avoided at all costs.

Wrong. They are essential for athletes. Sugar is a carbohydrate. Your carbohydrates are your primary energy source. Your body functions quite well with carbohydrates! Your brain needs carbohydrates to function normally. You do not need to go over board here. (Check out the *Macs* chapter.) In a nutshell, a few carbohydrates will help you prior to exercise and during competition. If you eat after training, carbohydrates will help you to fully recover. Carbohydrates are also protein sparing. They help you keep what you've earned.

Vitamins give you energy and enhance your strength and endurance.

This is not true. Vitamins provide no calories and can't be used as fuel. Energy is calories and vitamins do not provide calories. Only carbohydrates, fats, and proteins provide energy. The body will get rid of the vitamins it doesn't need. Only people who have vitamin deficiencies really need to take them. In modern times, it is hard to think anyone could be vitamin deficient. But it can happen. If you eat a correct and balanced diet you should be fine. The big word here is *if.*

Now let's be perfectly honest here. How many people do you know that actually eat a truly nutritious diet? I don't know about you but I don't know anyone that eats just like the government says they should. So taking a good multivitamin mineral tablet should be fine to ensure that you are getting at least the minimum that you need.

Excess protein will be used as energy.

True, but it is not as efficient as carbohydrate or even fat sources. Like all excess calories surplus protein can be stored as body fat. Not exactly what you want to do with your protein.

Athletes need more protein than the average couch potato.

This is true, but not an enormous amount. Currently the government recommends 0.8 grams of protein per kilogram of body weight. Research has shown that athletes may need somewhere between 1.2 to 1.8 grams of protein per kilogram of body weight or 0.5-1.0 grams per pound. Some researchers say up to 1.2 to 1.5 grams per pound. These may be a bit extreme. In general, we aren't talking about huge amounts.

Protein supplements are *not* necessary.

This is true. If you eat correctly they are not necessary. *If* is again the key word here. The catch is you must eat correctly. Eating should be taken as seriously as your training. All that being said protein supplements do provide a convenience. This is especially true when refueling the body for recovery after training. So the big question is: are you eating correctly?

People in the United States are the best fed people on earth.

Actually, we are probably the best over-fed people on earth. You can eat a box of donuts and get plenty of calories but you'll miss out on some key nutrients. It is easy to take a lot of things for granted. Do the right thing and eat the right things.

Taking extra vitamins will make me mature faster, become stronger, and improve athletic performance. Athletes need a lot of extra vitamins. As far as vitamins go, more is better!

Nope. Maybe just a little more than the average individual, but not a lot more. Some vitamins are actually toxic at high levels. Over supplementation has not been shown to increase the performance of already well-nourished athletes. Although vitamin and mineral deficiencies can weaken athletic performance, it is unusual for athletes to have such deficiencies. This is because they already tend to eat more than ordinary people. If you feel flat or spent it's probably because of overtraining, a lack of calories, carbohydrates, or sleep.

I do realize that although we live in a world that should have no nutritional deficiencies, they do exist. At times they exist even in overweight individuals. Proper nutrition is the key. For those not able to get in enough nutrients, supplementation should definitely play a role.

Vitamins can replace foods.

Nope. Your body needs the macronutrients (see the *Macs* chapter). Vitamins do not provide the protein, fat, or carbohydrate that your body needs. You can't live long on just vitamins.

Food cravings indicate a nutrient deficiency.

Nope. Unless I'm deficient in some type of nutrient found in chocolate and pizza. Usually food cravings come during a time of food restriction. Otherwise known as a diet. (Actually, some researchers believe that dark chocolate can provide some health benefit, however not in the amounts I like to eat.)

Chewing gum takes seven years to digest if you swallow it.

Nope. Although it is sticky it won't stick to the lining of your gut. And it will come out the other end!

Skim milk is less nutritious than whole milk.

Nope. Skim milk has the same 15 essential nutrients and in the same amounts as whole milk. This is true for 1% or 2% milk as well. The only difference is reduced fat in skim milk and less calories.

You can eat more food if they are low fat or fat free.

Not necessarily. Just because foods have less fat do not mean they have no calories. Remember, your weight comes from all calories, not just fat!

What you eat after the game does not matter.

It matters a great deal if you want to get the full benefit from the nutrients of your meal and recover optimally. Muscles are ready to receive a fresh supply of fuel during the first 15 minutes to a couple of hours after training. See the *You Can't Play if You Can't Move* chapter.

Sports drinks are no better than water.

False. Actually they are better than water during strenuous sports activity and for recovery afterwards. Read the *You Can't Play if You Can't Move* and the *Filling The Gas Tank* chapters.

PE Myths Wrap

Eat…and eat healthy.

> *"The mind is the limit. As long as the mind can envision the fact that you can do something, you can do it as long as you really believe 100 percent."*
> —*Arnold Schwarzenegger*

Sports Supplements:
Enhancement In A Bottle?

"Men give me credit for some genius. All the genius I have lies in this: When I have a subject in hand, I study it profoundly. Day and night it is before me. I explore it in all its bearings. My mind becomes pervaded with it. Then the effort which I have made is what people are pleased to call the fruit of genius. It is the fruit of labor and thought."
—Alexander Hamilton

Supplements are always a hot topic! People are always looking for the magic formula, magic pill, and magic wand to turn them into a champion. So, here is a general rundown on supplements. These tend to change often. This chapter doesn't include every single supplement available. What you see in the stores today may not be there next week.

What are supplements?

The U.S. Congress defines supplements in the Dietary Supplement Health and Education Act (DSHEA), which became law in 1994. The law defines supplements as products that are intended to supplement the diet, contains one or more dietary ingredients (including vitamins, minerals, herbs, amino acids), is expected to be taken as a pill, capsule, tablet, or liquid; and is labeled on the front as being a dietary supplement. The DSHEA requires companies to have the words dietary supplement on the labels.

Are they safe to take?

In some cases, yes. In others, no. There are even cases in which no one knows for sure. How about that for sitting on the fence? The U.S. Food and Drug Administration (FDA) checks out the safety of foods and medicines. The FDA does not check on supplements before they're sold.

Manufacturers of supplements do not have to provide the FDA with evidence that their products are effective or safe. However, they aren't allowed to market unsafe or ineffective products. Under DSHEA, once a supplement is marketed to the public, the FDA has the responsibility for proving that the supplement is unsafe before it can take action to restrict its use. Interesting huh?

The FDA has limited resources. The department looks first at public health situations. The agency can't do anything about supplements until it gets a complaint. This happened with the herb ephedra. The FDA pulled the supplement after it was linked to the deaths and poor health of a lot of people. Illegal products are those that may be unsafe or make false or misleading claims. This means you could be risking your health by taking unstudied or understudied supplements.

Are the claims on the bottle for real?

Supplement manufacturers can make three claims for their dietary products: health claims, structure or function claims, and content claims. Some manufacturers may describe the connection between a supplement and disease, the intended benefits of using the supplement, or the amount of nutrients available in the product.

Watch out for one-sided information from people with no formal training in nutrition, or from personal testimonials (health food store employees, friends, or chat rooms). Ask these people about their training in nutrition or medicine.

Some bottle labels say:

"This statement has not been evaluated by the FDA. This product is not intended to diagnose, treat, cure, or prevent any disease"

The law is to make sure the claims are accurate and honest. The FDA does not approve the claims. The law says if a label includes such a claim, it must state that the FDA has not tested its claim. The label must also state the product is not intended to "diagnose, treat, cure, or prevent any disease." Only a drug can legally make these types of claims.

Dietary supplements are not drugs. A drug *is* intended to diagnose, cure, treat, or prevent diseases. Before selling to the public, drugs must be studied to find out their effectiveness, safety and proper dosages. There was a study done on supplement ads in bodybuilding magazines (and they are full of ads!). Forty-two percent had no scientific backing for the claims made!

What is the *placebo effect?* (A new punk band?)

The *placebo effect* is a term used when a substance is taken, which shouldn't work, yet somehow it does. This is one way drug companies use to test new medicines. They give one group the real drug and the other group a "sugar" pill. Often, the "sugar" pill group has the same effect as the people taking the real drug! For the new drug or supplement to be considered effective, the experimental group must have better results than the placebo group.

This is important when discussing supplements because the placebo effect is probably high in this area. Don't get me wrong there is nothing wrong with a placebo effect. Adding a couple of pounds of muscle, inches on your chest, dropping a few pounds of fat, these can all be good things. The mind is a very powerful thing!

Should you check with the doctor before using supplements?

Excellent idea. Dietary supplements may not be risk-free at all times. While vitamin and mineral supplements are widely used and usually considered safe, you may want to check with your doctor before taking any supplements.

Do supplements help lose fat?

Not in any of the good studies that I've seen. Ephedra did work; however, it is now illegal as it has been associated with very serious side effects. The potential hazards found associated with Ephedra range from nervousness, dizziness, blood pressure and heart rate changes, chest pain, heart attack, stroke, seizures, and death.

Although it was slightly beneficial (except for the nervousness, dizziness, blood pressure and heart rate changes, chest pain, heart attack, stroke, seizures, and death part!), the same weight losses can occur with a good eating plan.

It seems like there are supplements coming out daily that say they will cut weight, drop fat, or make you a lean, mean fighting machine. This has been going on for years and will continue to do so. Most of them will also suggest you follow a diet of some sort. So you have to ask yourself, "What is working here: the diet or the supplements?"

Items like ginseng, kelp, and bee pollen, although often included in diet supplements, do nothing to help lose weight. The only safe, effective, and long lasting way to take off extra weight is a healthy eating plan and exercise.

What are vitamins?

Essentially, vitamins are nutrients you must get from food because your body can't make them. Vitamins are often added to foods to increase their nutritional value.

You need only small amounts. Thirteen compounds are classified as vitamins. The body can store Vitamins A, D, E, and K, the four fat-soluble vitamins. Vitamin C and the eight B vitamins are water soluble, so any excess is expelled when you go to the restroom. You must replenish these daily.

The lack of certain vitamins can cause a variety of medical conditions, even if other areas of the diet are perfectly fine. Some examples are scurvy (vitamin C deficiency), rickets (Vitamin D deficiency), reduced night vision (Vitamin A deficiency), beriberi (a deficiency in thiamine, vitamin B1), or pellagra (a deficiency in niacin, vitamin B3). There are other deficiencies but that is beyond the scope of this book. Essentially, if you eat right you won't have to worry about any deficiencies.

Are vitamin and mineral supplements OK?

The best way to get your vitamins is from real food. There is nothing wrong with taking a plain old multivitamin but if you're eating well you won't need one. Although, there is plenty of great food around you will still have some folks who just won't eat correctly. They may benefit from a supplement. Nothing wrong with that!

If you can't eat dairy products you might need a calcium supplement. Vegetarians often develop deficiencies in the B vitamin group. People who are on very strict diets can also benefit from supplementation. Talk to your doctor about any supplements you wish to take.

Is "natural" safer?

"Natural" doesn't guarantee something is safe or good for you. Elephant dung, poisonous mushrooms, sunburns are all natural, but none of them are good for you.

The FDA has seen some problems where manufacturers were buying herbs and other ingredients without first running sufficient tests. So these manufacturers had no way to determine if the products they ordered were actually what they wanted. The other potential problem is they had no way of knowing if the ingredients were free from any impurities.

Stuff to be careful about

It's late at night. You should be getting rest to recover from your training. You flip through the channels and get caught up in the latest, greatest nutritional supplement in the world. Do you order it? Probably not. You need to be on the lookout for fraud. These are usually products that don't work like they are described or don't contain what they are supposed to. The best-case scenario is they waste your money. The worst-case scenario is they can cause physical harm.

The types of claims made in their labeling and advertising often can identify bogus products. If the product is described as a "breakthrough," "magical," "a miracle cure," or "a new discovery" think more than twice before buying. If it were that great it wouldn't be sold late at night. It would be reported in prime time and used by highly regarded health-care professionals.

Other claims to be careful of include terms like "detoxify," "purify," or "energize." You'll have a hard time measuring these claims. Be careful of claims that state the product can fix a huge range of unrelated medical problems. No supplement can do that. And if they cured anything those supplements would then have to be classified as drugs. Any claims that a supplement is backed by scientific studies, but the manufacturer does not provide the studies, should be looked at with doubt. Sometimes, references are provided, but the studies can't be found or the studies are poorly designed or even out of date.

If any supplement manufacturer blames the medical profession, drug companies, or the government for covering up information about certain supplements they are probably not telling the truth. It is stupid to hold back information about potential cures. Too many people could benefit from great discoveries.

Do supplements create champions?

Nope. Good athletes are created first by their parents, then by their coaches, then by themselves by what they choose to do and not do.

Legal supplements will not take an individual who can't run, jump, or lift and turn them into someone who can run, jump and lift. Some athletes will take supplements believing they will improve performance. The placebo effect could be at work. The mind can be a very influential thing. There is nothing wrong with letting the mind help get your body in better condition.

Steroids

Anabolic steroids are manmade hormones similar to the male hormone testosterone. These are illegal and can be unsafe unless given by a doctor for a specific medical problem. See *The Bad Stuff* for more information.

Creatine

Creatine is a naturally occurring substance. It is not a steroid. It's been around for a long time. A French scientist discovered creatine in 1832. Way back in 1923, scientists found that the average person stores over 100 grams of creatine and 95% of that is in muscles. Creatine has been reported to have a "half-life" of six to eight weeks in the body. So what you may have in your system today will be half gone in about six to eight weeks. Some studies say taking it for only five days a month is enough. That's a lot less than what it says on the bottle. If athletes take it this way it'll cut the sales in the stores. And it's a huge seller in health food stores.

The American College of Sports Medicine (ACSM) has investigated hundreds of scientific studies on creatine. Their findings show creatine use can enhance exercise performance involving short periods of extremely powerful anaerobic activity. Examples of powerful anaerobic activity would be weight lifting, bodybuilding, sprints, football, and baseball. The use of creatine does not improve aerobic exercise performance, namely long distance running, long distance swimming, or long distance cycling. Creatine is the most popular supplement used by collegiate athletes, mainly in football, track and field, and wrestling.

The ACSM found a dosage of 20 g per day that most products suggest is unnecessary. A three-gram dose per day will reach the same level of increase in the muscle over the same time period. An athlete can expect to gain a few pounds in the first three to four days. This gain is likely caused by water retention associated with creatine loading in the muscle. A change in the muscle with the use of creatine does not copy muscle changes from exercise.

The ACSM also found there is no clear evidence in the studies that taking creatine would cause stomach upset, kidney problems or muscle cramping. However, some athletes do complain of stomachaches and muscle cramps. This is usually because they may not be hydrated enough or don't dissolve the creatine fully before taking it.

In one study, the subjects ingested 30 grams of creatine for six days. The person who gained the most weight was a vegetarian. It's been found that creatine uptake appears to be greatest in vegetarians. This is probably due to the fact that vegetarians have lower muscle creatine stores. It can also be possible that the vegan athletes may not be getting enough total calories. While some athletes show large increases in body weight, others may show very little change.

Creatine is unregulated. The long-term use of creatine has not been examined. There is no standard dose and there is a dose suggested on the bottles. It has not been studied enough, especially involving young athletes. Children and women who are pregnant or lactating should not take creatine (but why would they?).

Calcium

Calcium is a mineral that is necessary for certain body tasks, this includes proper blood clotting, production of strong bones, and proper nerve and muscle function. As a teenager your bones are developing rapidly and storing calcium. During this period almost half of all bone is formed.

Calcium is important in your diet because if your body does not get enough, it takes calcium from your bones. This can lead to a bone disease called osteoporosis. This disease occurs gradually. The bones become delicate and may break easily. Osteoporosis can lead to height loss because the spinal bones breaking. Some older people may develop a bent over back.

Girls are more at risk to develop osteoporosis. Teenagers between the ages of 9 and 18 should try for 1,300 milligrams of calcium per day. This is about equal to 4 calcium food servings daily. The best natural sources of calcium are dairy products. So get plenty of milk, yogurt or cheese. You can also get a good portion of calcium in enriched orange juice. Just read the package.

If you find that getting enough calcium from your food is difficult then you may wish to start taking calcium supplements.

Chromium

Chromium is a trace mineral that aids in the utilization of insulin. Well-controlled studies found chromium supplements did not increase muscle mass.

Chromium supplements are found to increase muscle growth in some animal studies. It hasn't done a thing for muscle size in humans.

Boron

At one time, boron was said to boost muscle size by increasing the male hormone testosterone. One study did find that 3-mg of boron a day increased serum testosterone. But this was in postmenopausal women! Not athletes! I don't think there are any postmenopausal women reading this and if they are in high school they would be your teachers not your fellow classmates! The study also found an increase of the female hormone estrogen. Not something the guys need to supplement in their diets.

In the only study of boron's effects on muscle mass in males, researchers examined the effect of daily boron supplements of 2.5 mg or a placebo for seven weeks in male bodybuilders. They found no difference between groups in lean body mass, total testosterone, and strength over the course of the seven weeks. So unless you are postmenopausal, don't waste your money on this stuff.

HMB (B-hydroxy B-methylbutyrate)

HMB does not stand for Huge Massive Body. It is made in the body and it can be found in some foods such as, citrus fruit, alfalfa sprouts, and catfish. It has been sold as a supplement in stores since the mid 90s and it's one of the most expensive supplements you'll find.

HMB is not an essential nutrient. In fact, the exact function of HMB in the body is not fully known. It is thought to prevent muscle breakdown, speed up recovery, and increase lean body mass. Scientific studies on HMB lend a little support that it can work as a growth-producing supplement during strength training. However, the amount of weight gain is low. Most high-level athletes do not believe HMB helps very much, especially when compared to creatine. We do not know the long-term affects of using this supplement.

Vanadium

Vanadium (sold frequently as vanadyl sulfate) is a non-essential trace mineral which supposedly has insulin-like effects. It has not been found to increase muscle size or athletic performance. Keep your money in your pocket.

Ginseng

Early research claimed that ginseng supplements improved exercise performance. However, more recent and better-controlled studies haven't shown any positive effect of either Chinese (Panax ginseng) or Siberian (Eleutherococcus senticosus) ginseng on performance. A slim maybe on this one.

Amino Acids

An amino acid is an organic compound containing an amino group (NH2), a carboxylic acid group (COOH), and any of various side groups, especially any of the 20 compounds that have the basic formula NH2CHRCOOH, and that link together by peptide bonds to form proteins or that function as chemical messengers and as intermediates in metabolism. What does this mean to you? Probably the same as it means to me…nothing!

So let's simplify this. Your body's cells use amino acids to make proteins. Basically, proteins are a "chain" of amino acids. Protein foods are broken down into amino acids before your body can use them. There are 20 amino acids with eight of them considered essential. An *essential* amino acid cannot be made by the body. These must be supplied in your food.

Two studies report that taking the amino acids arginine and ornithine along with strength training increase body mass and decrease body fat compared to a placebo. The claim is these particular amino acids stimulate the release of growth hormone and insulin. Both hormones are growth producing. However, there was no increase in serum insulin. There was an increase in growth hormone but only after about a 12 gram dose of ornithine (for a 154 pound athlete) was given. That is a huge amount of one amino acid!

The only study to use lower doses and report a considerable response was in 1981. A single total dose of 1.2 grams of lysine and 1.2 grams of arginine produced an increase in plasma growth hormone and insulin.

While some studies have found positive results other studies have not. A study following four days of taking arginine, ornithine, and lysine at two grams per day each did not increase growth hormone or insulin. Another study using male bodybuilders taking 2.4 grams of an arginine and lysine combination, a 1.85 gram of an ornithine and tyrosine combination, or a protein drink found there was no extra growth hormone release.

A study in 1997 found that 1.5 grams of arginine and 1.5 grams of lysine increased growth hormone. The increase was very small and didn't last long. The increase was highly unpredictable among those in the test. Taking these amino acids prior to resistance training did not affect the growth hormone response to exercise.

High levels of amino acids are known to cause stomach cramps and diarrhea. Some of these supplements are kind of expensive. It is unknown what can happen from the use of specific amino acids for a long period of time. It is possible that high amounts of one amino acid can affect how the body uses other amino acids. At this time, it is unclear if taking separate amino acids will help to enhance performance.

Another maybe on this one.

Tribulus Terrestris

Tribulus Terrestris. Don't worry how to pronounce it, you won't be asking for it any time soon. Most of the studies were animal studies geared towards finding out about an animals sex drive. Nothing we need to concern ourselves about here. Studies done on humans found no increase in testosterone output or exercise performance. Since tribulus does not appear to be useful for increasing hormone levels in healthy males or improving exercise performance you probably do not want to spend your allowance on this stuff.

ZMA

This is a combination of Zinc, Magnesium, and Vitamin B-6. If you become deficient in any of these you may see a decrease in performance in general. There is evidence that a number of diets can be deficient in all three. ZMA may also be helpful in recovery. ZMA supplements may have the potential to increase testosterone production and exercise performance but only in individuals deficient in any of these ingredients. In light of the new book *Game of Shadows*, ZMA may not be worth the paper the study was printed on.

Pro-hormone nutritional supplements

PHNS are said to increase testosterone levels and to enhance muscle size and strength. The most recent research has focused on androstenedione, androstenediol, and dehydroepiandrosterone (DHEA, sorry for the big words!). The reason for using PHNS is that chemically they are one or two steps away from testosterone. Studies show the following:

1. Taking DHEA doesn't increase blood testosterone in young healthy men.

2. Taking 100 to 200 mg of androstenedione doesn't change blood testosterone levels in college-aged men. Taking 300 mg androstenedione a day doesn't cause greater muscle size or strength with resistance training than just training alone.

Taking androstenedione and androstenediol can lower the good cholesterol. It is said this can equal a 10 to 15% increased risk for cardiovascular disease. Androstenedione can also increase blood levels of dihydrotestosterone (DHT), which is linked to baldness and prostate enlargement, both of which you don't want.

Energy drinks

Nutritionists look at energy strictly as calories. In other words, the food you eat provides you with the energy or fuel necessary to perform normal living or athletic events.

Some of the advertised energy drinks can have non-nutritional substances such as caffeine and ephedrine like substances. Many also include amino acids and lots of sugar. In a sense, this is "false energy". You don't want to become dependant on these. These could also be called "stimulant" drinks but the marketing and sales would probably not be as successful. These are not for rehydrating the body. One web site describes its drink as the equivalent of coffee and recommends drinking its product as one would their regular coffee intake. Definitely not for sports enhancement!

Nitric Oxide

This is a highly hyped and expensive supplement. It makes promises of huge gains in lean mass, long lasting muscle pumps, faster recovery, and increased strength gains. What you get in the bottle is not *nitric oxide*. What you get is the amino acid arginine (see amino acids above).

So, what can arginine do? Arginine plays a role in cell division, healing of wounds, removing ammonia from the body, and the release of hormones. It's found in foods like meat, poultry, dairy, and fish. The body can use arginine to produce nitric oxide, which can relax blood vessels. At times, arginine has been used to treat problems such as heart failure, impotence, and female sexual dysfunction. Does it work? It really depends on whom you talk to. Some people think it is great stuff, while others think it's a waste of money.

PE Supplement Wrap

If it sounds too good to be true or if the effects seem exaggerated or unrealistic—they probably are. New supplements come out all the time. Some will work, but most will not. Think before you spend.

> *"Take care of your body. It's the only place you have to live."*
> —Jim Rohn

You Can't Play If You Can't Move: Recovery, Recuperation and Immune System

"Regardless of what you do put in, every game boils down to doing the things you do best and doing them over and over again."
—*Vince Lombardi*

Recovery and Recuperation

Nothing can totally tank you like a hot, sweaty, grueling workout in July or August. So, how do we get ready for the next training session? Will eating fries and ketchup help in your recovery? Probably not.

Without proper recovery your performance will suffer. Not *may* suffer but *will* suffer. This can eventually lead to overtraining, decrease in performance, or injury.

Just what is recovery? Basically your body should be able to return to the way it was prior to exercise. You reduce muscle soreness and refuel your body with fluid, food and rest. The following are some suggestions to aid in recovery from training.

Don't stop moving!

Don't stop and rest right after strenuous exercise. The removal of waste products that build up in your muscles can be improved by steady, low intensity exercise for about 10 to 20 minutes. This cool-down phase can help reduce the stiffness and fatigue which often follows an intense workout. A cool-down phase is also important if you have to compete again in a couple of hours.

Fill up your muscles!

After exercise, your muscles are ready to be filled back up with nutrients. All athletes should start to replenish the body right after exercise. Don't wait for a few hours to pass. If you start immediately, your body will be ahead in the recovery game. And it's always better to be ahead of the game. A liquid meal consisting of a balance of protein and carbohydrates is best and within 15 to 30 minutes after exercise or competition. It doesn't have to be liquid but at that time liquid is more convenient. Whey protein is said to be quickly absorbed, so you may wish to try and have some in your first recovery meal. The most important thing is not the kind of protein you eat but that you get some. The fascinating thing about post exercise timing is you could take in a "lower quality" protein right after exercise and it will help you more in the long run than if you had twice as much of a higher quality protein hours later. The meals that follow should continue to have a variety of carbohydrates and proteins.

Some recent studies report adding carbohydrates and protein during training can actually enhance performance and recovery. The research isn't totally clear on this one as yet.

Studies show that a 154-pound athlete should take in 80 to 150 grams of carbohydrate within the first two hours following exercise to optimize the replacement of muscle energy (glycogen) stores. Another example suggests an athlete who weighs approximately 200 pounds should eat around 130 to 180 grams of carbohydrate following a workout.

Supplements

Nutritional supplements are not totally necessary but there is some evidence they may help a bit. Branched-chain amino acids (BCAA; leucine, isoleucine, and valine) may have protein sparing effects. This means they can help with recovery and keeping your muscle intact. However, some studies have found a higher ammonia production (waste products) when using these supplements. Carbohydrates are also protein sparing and cheaper. You can also get a ton of BCAA in a chicken breast.

Some coaches recommend taking Vitamin E and C. These antioxidants can help reduce the tissue damage that comes with exercise and enhance recovery. Also recommend by some authorities is glutamine (another amino acid) to aid in recovery.

Liquids

Water is lost in sweat especially on those hot, humid two-a-days. Replacing fluid is critical for recovery and peak performance. Fluids are needed to maintain your blood volume so you can deliver fuel to your muscles. Without an adequate amount of body fluid, you can't sweat enough to keep your body temperature from getting too high.

Replacement of fluids should be based on need. You should try to replace some of the fluid lost as sweat during exercise. You can tell how much sweat you lost by weighing yourself before and after training. However, you may not re-hydrate successfully unless you also replace the salt lost in sweat. (See the *Filling The Gas Tank* chapter for more details.)

Salt

Sweat is the salty liquid you lose while training. When you sweat, you lose water and minerals known as electrolytes. Mostly made up of salt or sodium chloride and potassium, electrolytes are important to replace during recovery. Drinking plain water during exercise and afterward can't totally replenish your stores of sodium. Salt must be replaced along with the water to prevent dehydration. This is especially true if you have to compete again in a few hours or during two-a-day training sessions. Consider using sports drinks during recovery for a quick and efficient way of replacing water, salt, and carbohydrates. If you are prone to cramping during intense exercise, you can add a little more salt on your food. This does not mean the whole shaker!

Streeeetttttccccchhhhhh

Stretching may help you recover from your training. It is also more productive if done at the end of training to get maximal benefit. If done early in training make sure you are warmed up. If you stretch your muscles too forcefully before warming up you can risk damaging them. It doesn't happen often but it can happen. Doesn't make a good locker room story. Some people claim stretching will minimize muscle soreness. This all depends on the person.

Heat, ice, massage, Oh My!

While you are exercising or competing, you can experience micro trauma or micro tears to your muscles. The tears cause inflammation and aching pain after strenuous training. Massage, cold packs, cold or hot whirlpool baths, alternating cold and hot whirlpool baths, as well as aspirin or other anti-inflammatory products can help lessen the pain and discomfort. Unfortunately, what works for one person may not work for another. So you'll have to try one until you find what works for you.

Sleep

Sleeping well can help you get physically and mentally prepared for your next workout or game. You can't perform your best if you aren't alert and are unable to focus on your activity. Occasionally, some competitors can get away with not sleeping enough. Eventually it'll catch up with them. They'll have a poor practice or performance or even an injury. Try to get around seven or eight hours of sleep each night. This will aid in recovery from training or competition.

Immune System

Your immune system consists of a group of organs and cells which defend your body against infection and disease. It helps keep you healthy and strong.

Long and hard workouts can cause a decrease in your immune systems' ability to handle problems. Studies show an increased risk of upper respiratory infection in endurance athletes a couple of weeks after competition. This is two to six times higher compared to couch potatoes. The risk for upper respiratory infection increases if the endurance athlete has frequent strenuous workouts along with lack of sleep, mental stress, malnutrition, or weight loss.

Nutrition is significant for positive immune system responses in athletes. These findings have substantial practical and public health significance.

Can athletes use supplements to counter immune changes?

This all depends on whom you talk to (or what they have to sell). Several supplements have been studied including zinc, dietary fat, plant sterols, antioxidants (vitamins C and E, beta-carotene, etc), glutamine, and carbohydrate. There is some evidence that a lack of some single nutrients can result in decreased immune reactions. In some instances, this is seen even if the decrease is relatively mild. Zinc, selenium, vitamins A, C, E, B-6, and folic acid all have some power over immune reactions.

Antioxidants

Antioxidants have received a lot of attention. So far, the evidence isn't 100% clear if they help to decrease disease processes as some claim. The antioxidant story begins with the body naturally producing chemicals (highly reactive, imbalanced molecules) called *free radicals*. These free radicals can cause damage or oxidation to your body's cells. This can weaken the body's defense against a variety of things including, aging, cancer, heart disease, and arthritis. You probably aren't worried too much about that yet (although you probably should).

Antioxidants act to reduce the damage of the free radicals. They help in the maintenance of a healthy immune system. Antioxidants may also assist in recovery or recuperation from intense training. This is a good thing for athletes since exercise naturally produces more free radicals. They include some vitamins and minerals (A, C, E, selenium).

You don't have to go out and buy a lot of this stuff. Antioxidants are abundant in fruits and vegetables, nuts, grains and some meats, poultry and fish. Recent studies have found that artichokes and red kidney beans were among the best sources of antioxidants. Other common foods would be cranberries, strawberries, broccoli, tomatoes, garlic, spinach, tea, carrots, blueberries, Russet potatoes, pecans, and even cinnamon. However, you can't use the excuse of eating a cinnamon bun just for the antioxidant value!

So far, antioxidant supplements haven't been found to be sport performance enhancers. Some studies have shown less soreness after exercise in individuals using vitamins C and E; however, other studies have found no benefit.

Antioxidants are a necessary ingredient for good health. At this time, no one can conclusively say how antioxidant supplements should be taken or how much. The government offers no guidelines for an amount of antioxidants you should eat. It has been found that vitamin C and beta-carotene are useful antioxidants in normal amounts; however, with mega doses they can become unsafe *pro-oxidants*. The long-term consequences of mega doses of antioxidants are unknown.

Carbohydrates

Studies in the '80s and early '90s found carbohydrates could maintain blood glucose levels, calm increases in stress hormones, and possibly reduce negative changes in immunity.

Glutamine

Glutamine has been in the press a lot. It's the most abundant amino acid in the body. Glutamine is mainly created and stored in your muscles. Glutamine is an amino acid that is classified as semi-essential because with normal circumstances the body can make enough by itself. Some studies found that glutamine helped when the body underwent stress like trauma, surgery, cancer, infection, and burns.

There is some evidence it helps protect against some of the apparent immune suppression found with overtraining. Some glutamine studies found an improvement in immunity and a decrease in infections after exercise and so it may help in keeping a healthy immune system. It may also help while recovering from training and competition. The studies are not totally consistent and more research is being done.

PE Rest Wrap

Recovery is usually one of the things left out of a good training program. Athletes, coaches, and parents should realize athletes need to recover from their activities. If the recovery is incomplete or nonexistent, the athlete will not reach his or her full potential.

> *"I am always doing things I can't do, that's how I get to do them."*
> *—Pablo Picasso*

If You Don't Know Where You're Going, You Won't Get There: Goals

"You can't hit a target you cannot see, and you cannot see a target you do not have."
—*Zig Ziglar*

Goals in athletics usually reflect an ambition to increase the number in the win column. This is a good idea for the team to be successful. Without goals, the win column will suffer.

The goals of athletes, just as in someone's personal life, is to move from one place (the present) to a better place (the future). If you aren't moving forward you are definitely moving backward. Neutral does not exist. The difference between where you are and where you want to be is *action*. Action needs to happen. Study and apply the following when developing your athletic goals:

- Goals need to have time frames. Another word for this is a deadline. A goal without a deadline is just a dream. So dream big! There is nothing wrong with dreaming. If you take action you'll have a chance to turn that dream into reality. Shoot for the stars! If you don't make the stars perhaps you'll land on the moon. And remember, there are footprints on the moon! You'll need short-term, midterm and long-term goals. You also need short, mid, and long-term deadlines. Your short-term goals should take you closer to your midterm goals. Your midterm goals should take you closer to your long-term goals. Think about what you want to accomplish as an athlete. What do you want to do by next week, by next month, in three months, in six months, in a year, or in five years?

- Goals need to be specific. It's better if they are written out in detail. The more specific your goals are the easier it is to see what you have to do to get them. You need to ask yourself some basic questions. What do you want to accomplish? Where is this going to take place? When will it happen? What are my

71

obstacles? What are my strengths and weaknesses? Who can help me? Why is this important to me? How will I start?

"The will to win is important, but the will to prepare is vital."
—Joe Paterno

- Goals need to be realistic. If you run a 40 yard dash in 8 seconds you won't hit 4.5 next week, but who knows what you can do with time, good training, and nutrition on your side!

- Goals need to be measurable. If you can measure it, it will get done. By being measurable you can record and watch your improvement. Keep track of your running times, the amount of weight you lift, the food you eat, etc.

- You have to be passionate about your goals. You have to want it. Things you are passionate about in life are the things that you will chase after and accomplish. These are things that get done. Things that don't get done are simply not important enough. Goals are essentially wants. Do you really want it bad enough?

"I find it fascinating that most people plan their vacation with better care than they do their lives. Perhaps that is because escape is easier than change."
—Jim Rohn

- Your athletic goals cannot contradict other personal goals or your personal philosophy of life. If some of your goals contradict others, they won't get done. People will see this and you will lose credibility. If you lose credibility with your team your integrity at school will soon suffer.

- Review your goals regularly. Daily is preferred but probably not realistic. Monthly is not enough. A weekly review will be enough to allow persistent focus. Continually ask yourself, "Are the decisions you make taking you closer to your goals or farther away from them?"

PE Goals Wrap

The real bottom line is you can't neglect the value of goal setting. This is something you must do. This isn't something you can try to do occasionally. And don't ever say, "I tried my best to set goals. It just didn't work." In the words of Jedi Master Yoda, "Do or do not. There is no try."

What To Do When You Don't Feel Like Doing: Motivation

"Nothing in the world can take the place of persistence. Talent will not. Nothing is more common than unsuccessful men with talent. Genius will not. Unrewarded genius is almost a proverb. Education alone will not. The world is full of educated derelicts. Persistence and determination alone are omnipotent. The slogan "press on" has solved and always will solve the problems of the human race."
—*John Calvin Coolidge*

Everyone at one time or another needs a little motivation. Let's first talk about plants. What do plants have to do with motivation? Read on!

A plant will grow as big as it can no matter where the seed lands. It has an *internal motivation* to grow. You never see a plant that only grows half way. Plants don't have a choice. They always perform to their max.

Humans…well humans are different. Humans usually will do what they need to do to get by. Occasionally, some humans will do more. These humans are motivated to do more. Those humans generally are in better health, make more money, and seem happier. But even humans who do more with their lives still need a little push. What separates the successful humans on and off the field from those who just skate along is the ability to choose and get motivated into action. Make no mistake this is a **choice**. And it is a choice that we all have to make over and over in our lives.

People ask "What good is getting motivated since it doesn't last long?" You have to be motivated over and over again. A guy named Zig Ziglar says baths are the same way. They don't last long either…but still it's a good idea to have one daily!

Motivation isn't a bad thing. Motivate yourself daily. You can't overdose on it. You can't get injured by it. It can't harm you. And it can be contagious. But it has to start somewhere. Why not let it start with you?

All people are motivated.

People make decisions and take action because of two feelings; pain and pleasure or some call it fear and happiness. Essentially, these are the same. If something is painful or you are afraid of it, you'll avoid it. On the other hand, if something feels good and makes you happy you try to find ways to keep it around.

This brings us to a story about an old man and his old hound dog being visited by his grandson. The grandson arrives in his new sports car at the old man's home. The old man is on the front porch rocking in a rocking chair. The dog is sitting by his side howling occasionally (*pay attention to the dog*).

The grandson shouts out, "Granddad! I finally graduated Harvard. I've got my MBA and I'm going to be successful and make a lot of money."

"That's mighty fine boy." The old man says rocking slowly as the old porch creaks. The old dog shifts his weight and howls.

"And I just bought this expensive sports car. I'm smart and did a lot of research and this is the best on the market! How do you like it?"

"Looks fine boy." The old man says unimpressed. The dog howls louder.

The grandson scrambles up the stairs of the porch to his grandfather. The old dog shifts his bottom and howls again.

The grand son, pulling a picture out of his wallet, says proudly "Granddad take a look at this picture. This is the best looking girl at school. I dated a lot and finally found the greatest girl on campus. It took me awhile but I found her. Yep I think I am just about one of the smartest guys to graduate Harvard!"

Just then the dog howls out like a lone wolf baying at a full moon.

The grandson looks annoyed at the dog. "Granddad just what is wrong with this dog?"

The old man looks slowly at the dog. Then glances up at his grandson and says, "Since you're so smart why don't you tell me!"

The grandson getting more aggravated now declares, "I have no idea!"

"He is sitting on a nail." The old man says flatly.

"A nail?" asks the grandson.

"A nail." repeats the old man.

Frustrated the grandson asks, "Well, why doesn't he move?"

The old man hesitates. He looks his grandson then the dog then his grandson again and says, "It just doesn't hurt bad enough yet."

When you get motivated enough you'll step into action. Don't wait till it "hurts bad enough". The dog had a choice. Was his choice the right one? What is your choice?

Do you need a break?

Honestly, do you need a break? Do you need a break from school, friends, parents, your sport, your nutritional plan? You may have been working hard and your sluggishness is your body and mind telling you that you need a break. This is where your champions are born. They are the ones who are honest with themselves. Is it a break you need or are you just getting a little slack? Sometimes we do need a break and sometimes we get a little lazy. Figure out which one it is and don't lose sight of your goals.

Change your eating routine.

Change your eating routine by planning a variety of meals, snacks and occasionally some junk food. At least if you plan for the junk food you'll have a better chance of not over loading. Just eat what you plan to and it won't feel like cheating because it isn't. I hate the word "cheating" when used with dieting anyway because it just cuts into you like a knife that you "cheated". If it is part of your diet it's just what you do. It's not cheating. And if you plan well, there is no harm in doing it. You can treat junk food like a reward for a job well done!

Feel it.

Motivation is emotional. Emotion is powerful. Think about how you felt at your most depressed time. You can almost feel the same way you did then. Now think about the time you were your happiest. Was it on the first date? Was it when you made the team? Was it when you made straight A's?

Your mind can create a great state for being motivated! If you are passionate about your sport you should become passionate about all aspects of your sport. When you feel the emotion you should turn it into action. The more action you achieve the more motivated you become. This is when you feel and become powerful. The action becomes momentum. You simply go with the flow. Now this doesn't mean slacking off, it means continuing to build on what you have already accomplished. Once you are in motion things tend to flow easier.

Get results.

Motivation is stimulated even more by results. If you work hard and smart, you'll get results. The more results you get the more motivated you'll become. You'll develop a sense of pride from your achievements. As your pride and self-esteem increase your motivation increases. It's a great circle to be in.

Stimulate your mind for motivation.

Hang around people who are motivating. Get away from people who bring you down. Sometimes, you may not realize you are in a downward spiral. Just look around you. You know the top performers and you know who isn't. Basically, you are the average of the five or six people you hang around with the most. (As you get older your salary will be about average of the five people you hang around with the most. You see this stuff doesn't stop in high school.)

Listen to CDs about motivation or about sports figures, military leaders, or businessmen who are successful. Listen regularly. Think about how you can use what they did in their lives to benefit yours. Let their success motivate you.

Read motivational books. If you want to know more about something the information is out there. It's easier to get information now than at any other time in history.

PE Motivation Wrap

Don't wait for someone to show up and motivate you. They might not show up! Go get it yourself!

"Everything you need for your better future and success has already been written. And guess what? It's all available. All you have to do is go to the library. But guess what? Only three percent of the people in America have a library card. Wow, they must be expensive! No, they're free. Probably in every neighborhood. Three percent!"
—Jim Rohn

Excuses, Excuses, Excuses

"Do...or do not. There is no try."
—Jedi Master Yoda

There are plenty of excuses not to eat right. Very, very few are valid. Why do we make excuses? It's simply a matter of trying to convince others (or more so ourselves) that we are right.

Just what are excuses anyway?

First of all, we have all made or continue to make excuses. That's one of the things that makes us human. You never see a plant make an excuse for not growing as tall as it could. If you plant a seed anywhere it will grow as large as genetically possible. It will do all that it can. That's what it does. That is its job. We could learn a thing or two from plants.

Can humans honestly say that? We waste time watching reruns on TV or babble on and on with phone calls to our friends about the reruns we just saw on TV. That time could better be spent on trying to better ourselves. No matter who you are or what you do, who you know, or how much money you have, you can always be doing something to better yourself. We're talking physically, mentally and spiritually.

There is no such thing as a good excuse. All excuses are the same. Excuses are just a pseudo reason for not following through or trying not to be held accountable for the situation. "He made me." "He looked at me funny." "She had an attitude." "I was tired." "It just slipped out of my hands." "I didn't mean to." "It just happened." "I got busy." "It's not my fault." "I didn't know I was going that fast." "My dog at my homework."

Most people don't want to think of themselves as "just making up excuses". But that's just what they are doing. We invent excuses to remove ourselves from blame or responsibility. There are a few good genuine excuses (death is always a good one) but the majority of them are wimpy, whiny, or just plain crap.

I know this can be tough to accept. Many of you are thinking that I may be full of crap. Many of you right now are dreaming up what you think are "good excuses" as you read this section. Hey, I understand. I didn't figure this out until I was a senior in college. Actually, to give credit where credit is due, it was pointed out to me by the head basketball coach at my undergraduate college. The coach was substituting for my regular Athletic Training professor. It was the only time I ever had a substitute teacher while in college. He said, "99.9% of the things that happen to you happen because you allow them to." There is so much to read into that. I continue to think about it to this day. Do I ever fall backwards? Sure. But with practice, I get better at taking responsibility for myself. And it does take practice. You already know that. It takes practice to get better at anything!

Since we have all been making excuses for years some of us have gotten pretty darn good at it. Sometimes we even believe our own excuses. Some of us are specialists and make excuse creation an art form. It's actually astounding at how much we can get away with just by having an excuse. What's more astounding or perhaps more appalling is how many of us actually believe what we are saying.

Just because you use the word "because" as in "I was running late *because* time got away from me." Doesn't mean it's a good or legitimate excuse. It isn't. Not at all. It's a total lack of respect to whomever you say it to.

If traffic is bad, you left too late. If you hit all the red lights, you left too late. If you overslept, you still left too late (or forgot to set your clock…another poor excuse).

If you were in a traffic accident or caught behind one—you win! That is a legitimate excuse! (If I show up five minutes after the post office closes it doesn't matter how much I plead about the traffic, it stays closed and it was my fault for getting there late.)

Excuses get you nowhere. And excuses concerning nutrition are just not legitimate in America. Eating correctly is not expensive, difficult, or dull.

"Success: Willing to do what the average person will not do."—Anonymous

But I don't like fruits and vegetables.

Again, there many things you'll do in life that you don't and won't like. There are things you like that are good for you. There are things you don't like that are good for you. The things to avoid are the things that are good, but are bad for you. (I'm sure you can come up with a list of these on your own.)

Fruits and vegetables provide essential vitamins and minerals, fiber, and water with little fat and no cholesterol. So eat 'em up!

But I don't like breakfast foods.

Not a problem. You don't have to eat the traditional things for breakfast. Your body doesn't really care if you eat chicken and vegetables for breakfast or ham and eggs. But, there is no excuse not to have breakfast. You're body has essentially been fasting for several hours. It needs fuel to function normally. So, don't skip your breakfast.

But I love sweets.

So do I. And you can continue to love them, just not all the time. You can have them. The key here is moderation. Don't make a meal out of several chocolate bars. You can switch to fruit. Some people are able to curb their sweet tooth by eating more fruit.

But I don't have time to cook.

Cooking takes time, no doubt about it. However, you don't have to create a gourmet meal. Use a microwave. The time it takes to cook is faster with a microwave. They can get a meal ready in a jiffy.

Cooking yourself also gives you more control over taste and nutrient content. It's usually cheaper too.

You have the time, believe me. Get up a few minutes earlier. Plan or prepare your meals in advance. Technically, you don't need to buy supplements. But for those of you who complain about lacking time, supplements are great for nutritious snacks. If time is your excuse you need to reevaluate your schedule. You may wish to reevaluate your goals as an athlete as well.

Looking for another excuse? Let me give you one...

But I don't know how to cook.

You didn't know how to walk when you were born either. You learned. You didn't know how to speak when you were born. You learned. You didn't know how to play a video game. You learned. You didn't know how to read. You learned. You didn't know how to play your sport. You learned.

You should get what I'm saying by now. But for anyone who may be acluistic (without a clue) here goes: pick up a book and read it. Ask someone that knows. They are out there. Do it. Sometimes you'll fail. Sometimes you'll succeed. But if you keep practicing you'll get better. Just like your sport.

But nutrition labels are confusing.

Some of the plays on the field are confusing too. Are you going to ask the coach to keep you out of certain plays because they are too confusing? Probably not. Unless you want to lose playing time. The more you study the labels, the less frightening they become. Nutrition labels help you make educated choices. And the right choices can place you above your competition.

"You have no control over what the other guy does. You only have control over what you do."
—AJ Kitt

But it's a chore to eat right.

It's not a too much of a task if the outcome is worth it. It really all depends on your attitude. You can have a bad attitude toward practice. You can have a bad attitude about your nutrition. Either way, your performance will be negatively affected. Without good nutrition you will never reach you full potential.

But eating correctly is boring.

Meals are boring only if you plan them that way. There is such an abundance of foods out there as well as supplements that boredom should not be a problem. If you plan your diet to be boring, guess what, it will be! Eat foods you like. Pizza is fine. Just don't eat the whole pie! And don't eat it every day! For the sake of argument, let's say eating correctly will be boring. A boring diet is much better than coming in last!

But it just isn't necessary.

Why did you buy this book if it isn't necessary? (Whoops. Birthday gift. Sorry.) Did you think when you opened it you would read, "Hey, it doesn't matter what you eat. You'll do OK?" If that were true this would be a mighty thin book.

Proper nutrition is necessary for everyone, but in particular, it is a necessity for athletes. This is especially true if the athlete wants to be and stay competitive.

> *"Do not let what you cannot do interfere with what you can do."*
> —*John Wooden: Basketball Coach, 10 NCAA Championships*

But it's just not fun.

Unfortunately, not everything you do is fun. That's just the way it goes. I'm sure some classes you have aren't much fun. Oh, by the way, losing isn't much fun either.

What you may want to do is ask yourself questions. Like "How can I make this fun?" You will come up with answers. That's just the way the brain works. You may not like the answers and you may not use them but there is always a way.

But what's the use? I'll never be Brett Favre.

No kidding. With that kind of an attitude you couldn't carry Brett's jock! It's not a matter of if you'll go pro. It's a matter of doing *everything* you possibly can to be the best you possibly can at everything you do. If you do everything right, you'll have a much better chance at getting to the next level.

But it's hard to keep up a good nutrition plan.

Actually, that's why they call it a plan. If you plan it right, it will be much simpler. Planning isn't much fun but its all part of the whole picture. Remember, your coaches have to plan your practices as well as come up with game plans against the teams you play. Planning is a huge part of success. Plan well and you're chances of success will increase.

I'll just wait until I get motivated.

You'll be waiting a long time. Motivation doesn't come to you. You create it inside by doing the things you feel are important. Anything you really want to do you are motivated to do it. If staying on top of your eating habits is not that important you simply won't do it. Keep in mind, without proper nutrition it can be difficult to perform at your best.

Oh yeah, don't wait for someone to come along and motivate you—they may not show up! Then what do you do? (Check out the *What to Do When You Don't Feel Like Doing: Motivation* chapter.)

But I can't afford supplements.

If you actually needed to have a lot of supplements then this excuse would ring true. However, you don't really need anything more than regular food. You can get all you need from your regular diet, if you plan it correctly. You do not have to depend on supplements.

I do realize that it may be truly difficult to get all of your nutrition from your regular foods. Supplements then have a place and can have a position in your nutrition plan. There is nothing wrong with using supplements. I think supplements are great. Supplements do provide nutrition. Keep in mind; this is more out of convenience than necessity.

But I think I'm doing fine just with what I'm doing now.

This may be true. You may be doing fine…for right now. This is a voice of someone who is stuck in the past and the present, but may not have much of a future. If the information is out there and especially if it is right in front of you (like right now), you should use it. It will help you reach your full potential.

But my parents aren't supportive.

Now, this is a good excuse. You may need to educate them on the value of good nutrition. Value doesn't only mean sports performance and the ability to recuperate sooner. Value is also the ability to live a longer and healthier life. Often, parents don't realize they aren't being supportive. And many times *you* may not realize how supportive they really are. Talk, ask, listen, and discuss intelligently.

PE Excuse Wrap

Excuses are dreadful. Eliminate all excuses. It will take practice until it becomes second nature just like on the playing field. Listen to Yoda: Do not try…Do! It will take perseverance but it can be done. There are lots of *Buts* in this chapter. Take the time to start kicking some.

Heat Illness, Hyponatremia, and Cramps: Oh My!

"I was made to work. If you are equally industrious, you will be equally successful."
—*Johann Sebastian Bach*

Heat Cramps

Just about everyone has seen the effects of heat cramps, or perhaps had them. You know—the painful spasms that squeeze your muscles and sometimes even take you out of the game. These are common in football, long tennis matches, cycling, running, basketball, and triathlons.

Not all cramps are alike. The cramps we're talking about are the spasms that appear to come from too much sweating, essentially from loss of body fluid resulting in dehydration. We aren't talking about your hand cramping up from taking too many notes in class!

What causes cramping?

The people most prone to heat cramps in sports seem to be the early, "salty" sweaters. You've seen them. They're the ones dripping before they leave the locker room. Sometimes the salt actually cakes up on their uniforms after a long practice. These athletes tend to lose more salt during exercise and dehydrate more than the light sweaters. Some causes of muscle cramping can be salt loss, dehydration, and muscle fatigue.

Picture a 225-pound football player during two-a-days in the blistering-hot August sun. He can easily lose a gallon of sweat during practice. In the sweat, the player can lose enough sodium to equal two or three teaspoons of salt. Smaller amounts of other minerals, namely potassium, calcium, and magnesium are also lost.

Sodium is important to maintain blood volume and it also helps nerves and muscles function correctly. Sodium reduction can decrease the coordination between the nerves and muscles. This obviously makes performance suffer.

To prevent cramping you should use just a little more salt. This does not mean to dump the whole saltshaker on your food! And of course, drink enough of the right fluids.

For most athletes, a balanced diet with a few salty foods, and correct hydration with water and a sports drink will be enough to reduce the risk of cramping.

Athletes who have a history of extreme cramping may need even more sodium. They can get this by adding a sprinkle or two of salt to a 16 to 24 ounce drink. Light stretching and self-massage of the involved muscles can aid in reducing the pain of a cramping muscle.

Sports drinks contain sodium to help reduce chances of muscle cramping. There are several sports drinks on the market. Be sure to read the labels. Water is not the best choice on really hot, humid days.

Muscle soreness

Muscle soreness can come from a number of activities. It generally happens from actions that resist gravity. Examples are running down a hill or stairs, slowly lowering weights, and the downward part of push-ups and sit-ups. These actions tighten the muscles during a muscle lengthening phase. This action is called *eccentric* or *negative*. All activities involve eccentric movements but are chief in the actions mentioned above.

DOMS or delayed onset muscular soreness usually occurs within 12 to 48 hours after exercise. The most popular explanation for muscle soreness is the build up of lactic acid. However, we've known for over 15 years that lactic acid doesn't cause this type of muscle soreness. Lactic acid has been largely discredited because it can be out of your body in an hour or so. It is now thought that micro muscle damage from exercise is the cause of muscle soreness.

Treatment

Treatments for muscle soreness include: light stretching, sports creams, ice packs, heat, and hot or cold whirlpools. These treatments can provide short-term relief. The use of anti-inflammatory drugs like aspirin or ibuprofen may provide some relief as well, but not always. Light exercise has been found to help in some cases.

This means just going through the motions with minimal amount of discomfort but not full out.

Minimizing soreness

Athletes with sore muscles will not be able to practice or perform at their best. One reason is because the sore muscles will have less strength, essentially caused by the pain or discomfort. A training program should gradually increase the intensity and duration over a few weeks to prevent or minimize soreness and to reduce the risk of injury. Plyometrics, downhill running, and negatives have no place in the beginning phase of training.

> *Adversity causes some men to break; others to break records.*
> *—William A. Ward*

Heat Illness

Everyone should be aware of the potential problems that can occur while exercising in the heat. Athletes should especially be aware of recognizing, preventing, and treating heat illnesses (dehydration, cramps, heat exhaustion, heat stroke, and hyponatremia).

Individual factors can contribute to heat illness such as: not being used to the heat, poor fitness level, high body fat, dehydration, over hydration, illness, stomach upset, lack of salt, inadequate food intake, motivated athletes (those who work through the pain), and athletes who are quiet or hesitant to report problems.

Other factors also need to be addressed, including: exercise intensity and length, frequency, time taken for rest breaks, exposure to heat and humidity during previous days, clothing, staff awareness concerning heat illness, and plans to assure satisfactory fluid intake. Heat illnesses can be avoided by education and the presence of a medical team or at least an emergency plan.

Dehydration

When athletes do not replace fluids during exercise, they can become dehydrated. Mild dehydration (less than two percent body weight) is common because athletes cannot always balance fluid intake with fluid loss during practice or competition. However, even mild dehydration can decrease performance.

Signs of dehydration can include dry mouth, thirst, irritability, general discomfort, headache, lack of interest, weakness, lightheadedness, cramps, chills, vomiting, nausea, fatigue, and diminished performance.

Preventing dehydration

Maintaining normal hydration is the key to preventing heat illness. Athletes should weigh themselves before and after practice or competition. This is especially true if you must train in the heat. Athletes should not be allowed to practice if their total body weight-loss is greater than two percent of their baseline body weight (example: four pounds for a 200 pound athlete). Athletes should begin each training period properly hydrated (within two percent of their baseline body weight) and should have easy access to fluids during and after practice.

Treating dehydration

The athlete should be moved to a cool location and re-hydrated gradually with a sports drink containing carbohydrates and electrolytes.

Return-to-play issues for dehydration

Continued participation is okay if dehydration is mild (less than two percent of the baseline body weight) and the athlete has no symptoms. The coaching staff should do occasional checks to ensure proper re-hydration and no reoccurrence of symptoms.

Heat Exhaustion

Heat exhaustion is a type of heat illness that can come from exhausting exercise and heat stress. It occurs when the body can no longer get rid of heat successfully because of extreme outdoor conditions or increased body heat.

Symptoms can include fatigue and dizziness, dehydration, passing out, extreme sweating, turning pale, headache, nausea, vomiting, diarrhea, stomach cramps, and constant muscle cramping.

Treating heat exhaustion

Get yourself to a shaded or air-conditioned place and remove any clothing you don't need and any equipment as well. The books say to cool yourself until your rectal temperature is less than 101 degrees. (I don't know who you'll get to measure that one!). Also lie down with your legs elevated. Re-hydrate yourself with cool water or a sports drink. Some people may not be able to tolerate drinking any fluids. This is when you get yourself to the emergency room.

Return-to-play after heat exhaustion

You should not have any symptoms. You should also be fully re-hydrated and cleared by a doctor before returning to play. Gradual return to full training or competition is recommended.

Heat Stroke

Heat stroke is the most severe form of heat illness. If the weather is hot enough a heat stroke can occur even in people who are not exercising. Athletes who have heat stroke after exercising in hot weather may or may not be sweating. Strange but true. A person with heat stroke will have a very high temperature (104 degrees or higher), may be hallucinating, unconscious, or even having seizures. Other symptoms can include vomiting, diarrhea, headache, dizziness, weakness, increased heart and breathing rates, decreased blood pressure and dehydration.

Call 911!! These people need to have their temperature reduced fast. They must be taken to the hospital as quickly as possible. Since body organs can fail during heat stroke the athlete may stay in the hospital for observation.

Return-to-play after heat stroke

Athletes should avoid exercise for at least a week after release from medical care. They should return gradually to full practice after being cleared by a physician.

Hyponatremia

Sometimes people can take dehydration prevention too far. By mistake they can drink way too much water. Drinking too much water can lead to over-hydration or hyponatremia. Hyponatremia is considered rare. It is usually seen in serious endurance events like the Iron Man competitions, marathons, and ultra-marathons. However, it can be very dangerous and athletes should be aware of the problem. Hyponatremia is also known as water intoxication.

The risk of hyponatremia is increased during long athletic events or practices. Especially when sodium lost in sweat is not balanced by sodium intake. Hyponatremia can also occur in athletes involved in prolonged exercise of over five to six hours, and who are *not* over-hydrated, but don't put back the sodium they lost in sweat.

Athletes who drink too much water after exercise can further reduce sodium and chloride levels, which can lead to further electrolyte depletion and possible over-hydration. To completely re-hydrate you must replace water and also sodium and chloride.

Symptoms of hyponatremia

The symptoms of hyponatremia are very similar to the symptoms of other heat illnesses. Heat illnesses can be deadly. If you or someone you know has symptoms it is important to get medical attention immediately. The most common symptoms are fatigue, lightheadedness, weakness, cramping, nausea, headache, confusion, fainting, and in severe cases seizures and coma. Although rare, this is nothing to play around with.

Hyponatremia can be avoided if fluid consumption does not go beyond fluid loss and if the athlete takes in enough sodium.

Treating hyponatremia

If hyponatremia is suspected, carry out measures to cool the athlete. Remove or loosen clothing and equipment. Fan and place cool water on the skin and get the athlete to the hospital!

Return-to-play after hyponatremia

Medical clearance is necessary in all cases.

PE Heat Wrap

You don't mess with heat illnesses of any kind. Having more knowledge about these things gives you an advantage over your opponents and allows you to train safely.

"It's at the borders of pain and suffering that the men are separated from the boys." *Emil Zatopek; Czech runner, 3 Olympic Gold Medals, first to run 10K under 29 minutes.*

Timing: Before, During, and After

"If you don't do what's best for your body, you're the one who comes up on the short end."
—Julius Erving; "Dr. J"

Most high school students skip a meal or two here and there. Just about everyone does. Doing this once and a while won't be totally destructive. However, it won't help performance either. As an athlete, if you aren't doing something to help your performance you aren't going to improve. And your competition may be doing just a bit more than you. Nutrition should be a priority before and after exercise (and occasionally during). In general, the training diet in sports should be high in complex carbohydrates (55 to 60% of total calorie intake), sufficient protein (15 to 25%), and fat (15 to 25%).

Pre-exercise meal

A pre-event meal serves two purposes. First, it keeps you from feeling hungry before and during the game. Second, it helps to maintain levels of energy for the muscles during exercise.

Eating before exercise isn't easy for some athletes. Food that remains in the stomach during training or competition can cause heartburn, upset stomach, nausea, and sometimes vomiting. A good recommendation is to eat a meal a couple of hours before exercise or competition.

The ideal pre-exercise meal should be high in carbohydrates, moderate in protein and low in fat. Carbohydrates digest rapidly and the body tends to use more carbohydrates during exercise. Protein and fat take longer to digest. Meals high in fat can cause stomach upset, gas, and bloating.

Hydration during exercise

Most people don't think of fluid replacement as a meal during exercise, but it is. And it is just as important as the before and after meals. During practice or games, athletes need to drink water and sports drinks to avoid dehydration and provide energy for the working muscles. (See the *Filling The Gas Tank* chapter for more details.)

Post-exercise meal

After-exercise nutrition is extremely important. Breakfast and the after training meal are your most important feed times. The correct post-game meal replenishes your muscles for your future events. Muscles are most receptive to recovery and rebuilding during the first 30 minutes after workouts. Males have a longer window of time; one to three hours. Females have a shorter window (within 60 to 90 minutes) of time to maximize their recovery. All athletes should try to follow these guidelines:

1.   Eat within 30 minutes after exercise. Then eat small meals around 90 minutes to two hours later. The first meal could be a sports drink that has both carbohydrates and protein. This doesn't have to be a huge meal. About 200 calories from carbohydrates each time is enough.

2.   Be sure to drink water or a sports drink after a workout or game. Weigh yourself and drink about two to three cups of fluid for each pound lost during exercise.

PE Timing Wrap

Overall nutrition is very important. However, the timing of nutrition is what separates the champions of yesterday from the champions of tomorrow.

"Boys, there ain't no free lunches in this country. And don't go spending your whole life commiserating that you got the raw deals. You've got to say: 'I think that if I keep working at this and want it bad enough I can have it.' It's called perseverance."
—*Lee Iacocca; Former President Ford Motors, Former CEO Chrysler*

Surviving Two-a-days

"The difference between the impossible and the possible lies in a man's determination."
—*Tommy Lasorda; Major League Baseball, Player, Manager, Hall of Fame*

You won't believe it, but some schools are actually doing three-a-days! These types of workouts are most often seen as a part of pre-season conditioning in football. Other sports, like swimming and Olympic weight lifting do this type of training as well. The extra practice time seems to help physical conditioning and gives time for strength training and technique improvement.

Potential for injuries can increase during two-a-day workouts. Muscle pulls, strains and sprains, and joint injuries lead the list of injuries for two-a-day training. Other problems include emotional stress, sleeplessness, upset stomach, diarrhea, more colds and flu type symptoms, as well as dehydration issues or heat related illnesses.

In football, players are under further stress because of the heat and humidity of the hot summer practices. It's not just football players in the summer but also marching bands, cheerleaders, and even the coaches!

The thing is you're supposed to work up to training like this, not just jump right into it. Most schools have some type of conditioning program but not all. Sometimes common sense just isn't that common. Use your brain to help you survive those two-or three-a-day training sessions. If your brain is missing, hang around with someone who has one that works! And follow these suggestions:

• Start some conditioning work in the heat a few weeks before you start your official practices. This will get your body a little used to the heat and humidity. As you get accustomed to it your body tends to cool off better.

• Have only moderate workouts during hot and humid practice conditions. Two-a-days could be done during cooler times (early in the morning or late in the evenings).

- Before, during, and after practice drink plenty of fluids. A simple (but not precise) way of checking for proper hydration is by looking at the color of your urine. The lighter the color the better hydrated. Long workouts mean you'll need more frequent fluid breaks. A sports drink can provide energy, electrolytes, and fluids to help improve or sustain performance. Water cannot. Try to have eight to ten ounces of fluids every 15 to 20 minutes.

- Don't drink soft drinks, fruit juices, or drinks with caffeine. They won't do the job.

- Try to weigh yourself before and after training. For every pound of weight lost, you should try to drink about 15 to 20 ounces of fluid to help with rehydration and recovery.

- Rest! Try to get in the shade or inside during breaks. You'll lose more fluids and increase your temperature if you rest in the sun.

- Wear loose fitting clothes. Preferably the newer high tech type that allows your body to breathe. Experienced runners are the gurus in this department.

- Get plenty of rest and sleep after training. (Don't forget to do your homework!)

PE Two-A-Day Wrap

Rehydrate, recuperate, rest, and repeat!

"Apply yourself. Get all the education you can, but then, by God, do something. Don't just stand there, make something happen!"
—Lee Iacocca

Pick A Sport. Any Sport: Specific Sport Examples

"It's not necessarily the amount of time you spend at practice that counts; it's what you put into the practice."
—Eric Lindros; National Hockey League

Different sports sometimes require different nutritional needs. What the cross-country runner needs to eat for performance differs from a football offensive lineman. These are some suggestions for a few sports.

Wrestling

Amateur wrestling is an ancient sport. And it's the ultimate contact sport—a clash between two humans who win or lose—afterwards you know you have been in a battle. It has been described as a chess match on a mat. One wrong move and match over.

Wrestling is unique because the athletes generally cut weight for the weigh-in. You don't see this in football or track. Because of this wrestlers must carefully adjust intakes of energy: carbohydrate, fat, and protein. The smart wrestlers refuse to lose a lot of weight to compete in low weight classes. It can be unhealthy, especially for growing teens, to lose body weight quickly by dehydration or starvation.

Losing weight rapidly can have negative reactions and hurt performance. Mood disturbances can weaken the ability to focus. Extreme calorie reduction can reduce energy and can lead to overtraining. Increased fatigue can be a result of a decrease in blood volume. This can come about with fluid restriction. Restricting fluids can indirectly raise body temperature higher than normal during training. The athlete is then at a higher risk for heat illness.

In college and in some high schools, restrictions on weight cutting have generally helped wrestlers maintain good health. The smartest coaches and wrestlers watch what they eat day-to-day to prevent the need for huge and hurried weight loss.

The athlete and coach should figure out a reasonable competing weight. A proper nutrition plan should then focus on maintaining weight to achieve peak performance. Simply choose a training diet which is high in complex carbohydrates (55 to 60% of total calorie intake), protein (15 to 25%), and fat (15 to 25%). Drink to stay hydrated (see the *Filling The Tank* chapter). There are some competitors eating up to 75% carbohydrates and doing very well with competition and recovery.

Prior to competing, eat a high-carbohydrate, easily digested snack or meal. Eat or drink carbohydrates to replenish energy stores after practice or matches. Eat small or moderate sized meals every three to four hours. This will help control appetite, keep the body fueled, and reduce over eating.

During wrestling tournaments, competitors must try to recover from each match to compete successfully throughout the event. The goals during the recovery period are to restore muscle glycogen by eating carbohydrates and replace fluids as much as possible. This can be done more conveniently with sports drinks or lighter meal replacement bars. To minimize fullness avoid high fiber and high fat foods. They empty slowly from the stomach. Don't drink carbonated drinks because they can cause a bloating sensation.

Tennis

Tennis is a power sport. You need to fuel the power with proper nutrition. This will allow you to move quickly and deliver commanding forehands, backhands, and serves.

The season is held during some of the warmer months with high heat indexes and hot courts. Dehydration and heat illness are primary concerns in tennis. Adequate hydration is necessary to prevent any type of heat related problems (see the *Filling the Tank* chapter). The tennis-training diet should be high in complex carbohydrates (55 to 60% of total calorie intake), enough protein (15 to 25%), and fat (15 to 25%).

On tournament days, athletes should focus on high-energy (carbohydrate) foods and fluid replacement. Food and fluid replacement timed properly before and after multiple competitions will give the athlete the best advantage against exhaustion.

Pre-match meals should be made of food familiar to the athlete. This will insure the athlete has no worries of hunger or stomach upset. Carbohydrates are necessary to supply energy for the muscles during long match play. The meal should be quickly digested and not too high in fiber or fat. Good examples of pre-match meals rich in carbohydrates are pasta, bread, fresh fruit, energy bars, and sports drinks. These pre-match foods are also important during multiple match play. Caffeine containing drinks, such as tea, coffee, and soft drinks should be avoided right before and after matches. These drinks can cause further fluid loss through increased urine production. Drink enough fluids throughout the day so urine is a light, pale yellow color before starting a match. Athletes should try to drink every 15 to 20 minutes during play.

After the match, athletes should consume carbohydrates within 15 to 30 minutes. This can start immediately after the match with a sports drink. Within a couple of hours, replace 100 to 150% of the fluid lost or around 15 to 20 ounces per pound of weight lost during play. Try to have a high-carbohydrate meal with some protein foods within 30 minutes after play to maximize muscle recovery.

Football

"The price of success is hard work, dedication to the job at hand, and the determination that whether we win or lose, we have applied the best of ourselves to the task at hand."
—*Vince Lombardi*

Football is not a contact sport, it's a collision sport. It combines strength, power, skill, and speed. Any of these can suffer if the player is not nutritionally prepared. Football is interesting from a training aspect in that different positions should train in a different way. Linemen do not need to train like wide receivers. While both play the game of football their physical requirements are totally different. However, from a nutritional standpoint, they can get by from almost the same diet make up. The lineman may have to eat more calories. The receivers may need a few more carbohydrates to keep them running. In general, their nutritional plans can be comparable. Obviously their physical conditioning will be different.

Not drinking enough and not eating enough are common nutritional mistakes football players make. Often, they are guilty of eating too much fat and protein but not enough energy producing complex carbohydrates. This is especially true at the high school level.

Football players have goals on the field and in the weight room. They should also have daily nutritional goals to maintain performance. Drinking at regular times and keeping energy levels high by eating smaller meals or snacks every three to four hours will keep most athletes primed and ready to play. Care must be taken during the two-a-days taking place in the hot summer and fall months.

High school players have three important meals. Breakfast literally "breaks the fast" of sleeping to fill the energy reserves for the beginning of the day. You must eat lunch. I repeat you must eat lunch. In general, school lunches will have something nutritional prepared. It may not taste good but that doesn't matter because you are fueling your body, not your taste buds. This is important for high school players because practice is only a few hours after lunch. You need to be fully fueled, not only for games but for the practices as well. The third most important snack or meal is after training or competition.

In general, the training diet is similar to other sports: high in complex carbohydrates (55 to 60% of total calorie intake), protein (20 to 25%), and fat (20 to 25%). Drink enough fluids throughout the day so urine is a light, pale yellow color before practice or games. Athletes should try to drink every 15 to 20 minutes during the game or practice and during timeouts or halftime. Sports drinks will give players carbohydrates and sodium to help minimize cramping and dehydration.

After practice or a game, athletes should consume carbohydrates within 15 to 30 minutes. Adding a little protein at this time will help with the rebuilding process. Within a couple of hours replace 100 to 150% of the fluid lost or around 15 to 20 ounces per pound of weight lost during play. Try to have a high-carbohydrate meal with some protein foods within one to two hours after play to maximize muscle recovery.

Baseball

"Baseball is 90% mental, the other half is physical."
—*Yogi Berra; Major League Baseball Player, Manager, and in the Hall of Fame*

If you really think about it baseball is one of the most sedentary sports around. In the best games nothing much happens. A guy standing up throws the ball to another guy squatting down. Another guy tries to hit the ball. Most of the time he's unsuccessful. And all the other guys on the team are either standing around on the field or sitting in the dug out watching! The winning team is usually the one in which the guys playing catch are more successful than the guys trying to hit the ball. The more completed catches the less the whole team has to do.

While that may describe most of the game it leaves out other aspects of the game like hitting, base running, running for the ball, and game management. The baseball player, while most of the time not performing, has to be ready in a split second to execute at his or her maximum ability. So the training can be more intense than the game itself.

High school baseball players have three most important meals. Breakfast literally "breaks the fast" of sleeping to fill and fuel the beginning of the day. Some baseball programs have early training periods. Still, eat something but nothing heavy or you'll lose it…all over you, your friend, or the field! You must eat lunch. You must eat lunch. I repeat…you must eat lunch. Your schools lunch may not taste good but that doesn't matter because you are fueling your body not your taste buds. This is important for high school players because practice is only a few hours after lunch. You need to be fully fueled not only for practices as well as games. And practices in baseball are usually tougher than the game itself. The third most important snack or meal is after training and competition.

In general, the training diet is similar to other sports: high in complex carbohydrates (55 to 60% of total calorie intake), protein (15 to 25%), and fat (15 to 25%). Drink enough fluids throughout the day so urine is a light, pale yellow color before practice or games. This is especially true during practices in the spring or summer. Athletes should try to drink every 15 to 20 minutes during the game or practice. Sports drinks will give players carbohydrates and sodium to help minimize cramping and dehydration.

Basketball

A psychology teacher just completed a lecture about mental health. He then began to give an oral quiz to the class. Speaking about manic depression, the teacher asked, "How would you diagnose a patient who walks back and forth screaming at the top of his lungs one minute, then sits in a chair crying like a baby the next?" A young man in the back of the room raised his hand and answered, "A basketball coach?"

Basketball requires agility, balance, coordination, and some strength under the boards. It doesn't take a lot of strength to shoot the ball, but it certainly does when running into big, tall people guarding the hoop. While football is a collision sport, basketball is definitely a contact sport. It can also be intense on the cardiovascular system if you play on a fast breaking team or guarding against one.

Basketball players are fueled very similar to some other sports. High school basketball players have three most important meals. Breaking the fast of sleep, better known as breakfast, fuels the beginning of the day. Some basketball programs have early training periods. Still eat something but nothing heavy or you'll lose it...all over you, your friend, or on the court! Not a pretty sight or smell. You must eat lunch. You read that correctly! You must eat lunch. This is important for high school players because practice is usually only a few hours after lunch. You need to be fully fueled for the games and also for practices. The third most important snack or meal is after training or competition. In general, the training diet includes: high complex carbohydrates (55 to 60% of total calorie intake), protein (15 to 25%), and fat (15 to 25%).

Athletes should try to drink every 15 to 20 minutes during the game or practice and during timeouts and personnel changes. Fatigue from dehydration is the most common nutritional problem. Drink enough fluids throughout the day so your urine is a light, pale yellow color before practice or games. Sports drinks will give players carbohydrates and sodium to help minimize cramping and dehydration.

Basketball players have goals on the court and should also have daily nutritional goals for peak performance. Drinking at regular times and keeping energy levels high by eating smaller meals and snacks every three to four hours will keep most athletes primed and ready to play. Eat foods you are familiar with. Never try a new food on game day. If you have never had a jalapeno pepper in your life, game day is not the time to start! If you wish to experiment with foods do it on practice days. Basketball players should try to eat two to four hours before the game to give their body enough time to digest the food. Meals should get smaller as the game or practice time grows near.

After practices or games athletes should have some carbohydrates within 15 to 30 minutes. Having a little protein at this time will help with the rebuilding and recovery process. Within a couple of hours, replace 100 to 150% of the fluid lost or around 15 to 20 ounces per pound of weight lost during play.

Volleyball

The nutrition goal for volleyball players is to eat enough to fuel practice and game conditions. This means an adequate amount of food in the form of carbohydrates, proteins, and fats. You need about of 130 grams of carbohydrates a day to maintain a fully functioning brain, but athletes need more because of their activity levels. To get enough carbohydrates the volleyball diet should focus on whole grains, fruits, vegetables and dairy products. In general, the training diet should include: high complex carbohydrates (55 to 60% of total calorie intake), protein (15 to 25%), and some fat (20 to 25%). Carbohydrates are the primary fuel source needed during performance and also recovery. Protein is used to maintain muscle and rebuild. Essential fats round out a good athletic diet.

The purpose of the pre-game meal is to bring up energy stores for the players to enter a match with a full tank of fuel. The meal should be eaten about two or three hours before the warm-up session. This is no time for experimentation. If you want to experiment with different foods do this before practice or during conditioning sessions. The pre-game meal should be high in carbohydrates, a moderate amount of protein, followed by a low amount of fat. The more fat and protein you take in the slower the digestive process. You don't want to be bloated on the court. Gradually drink about 24 ounces of water or a sports drink and you're good to go.

Maintaining fluid levels and reloading the energy you use are the two nutritional factors necessary for success. This can be achieved by using sports drinks during the match. The recommended amounts during the match are about six to eight ounces of fluid every 15 to 20 minutes. Water is a good fluid option but it won't replace the energy burned during the match. Sports drinks at this time are a better choice. Tournaments will require rehydration between games for perfect performance.

A post game meal or snack is very important for recovery. Unfortunately, athletes can be too tired to eat or emotionally drained after a loss. However, this is the time when the body is hungry to restore energy for the next match or practice. You should eat this meal within 15 to 30 minutes after competition.

Soccer

General health and sports performance is dependant not only on how much you eat but what you eat. Three meals a day will not fuel the soccer player. Smaller meals throughout the day are necessary for proper fueling and performance. You need a certain amount of food just to get up and do every day things. You need a bit more for peak performance on the field. And you need even more to recover from the practices and games.

It is estimated that a soccer player runs the equivalent of 10 to 13K during a game. Without enough energy stored, performance will suffer. A low fitness level isn't always the reason players run out of gas in the second half. It could be something as simple as not eating enough carbohydrates. If you don't put gas in the car you don't get far!

The soccer training diet should be high in complex carbohydrates (55 to 60% of total calorie intake). Protein and fats should be of moderate amounts (15 to 25%). Drink to stay hydrated (see the *Filling the Tank* chapter).

Pre-match meals should be made from foods familiar to the athlete. This will insure the athlete has no worries of hunger or stomach upset. Carbohydrates are necessary to supply energy for the muscles. The meal should not be too high in fiber or fat. This will only slow the digestive process and slow you down on the field. Good examples of pre-match meals rich in carbohydrates are pasta, bread, fresh fruit, energy bars, and sports drinks. Caffeine containing drinks, such as tea, coffee, and colas should be avoided right before and after matches. These drinks can cause further fluid reduction by increasing urine production. Drink enough fluids throughout the day so urine is a light, pale yellow color before starting a match. Athletes should try to drink every 15 to 20 minutes during play.

After matches players should have carbohydrates within 15 to 30 minutes. Adding a little protein at this time will help with the rebuilding and recovery process. Within a couple of hours replace 100 to 150% of the fluid lost or around 15 to 20 ounces per pound of weight lost during play.

Swimming

Swimming performance like other sports depends upon a number of factors. These include motivation, training, nutrition and your parents (heredity). Picking your parents can't be done, however you do have some control over your training, nutrition, and motivation. If you don't feed yourself correctly your training and motivation can suffer. Swimmers need a balanced diet which contains enough nutrients to keep up with normal daily activities, fuel for training, racing, and recovery.

Every set of every training session and dryland workout requires energy. Carbohydrates are the primary food source for swimmers. They are also the most efficient energy source used by the body for fuel. The greatest amount of calories per day (55 to 60%) should come from carbohydrates. So the training diet should include: high complex carbohydrates, protein (at 15 to 25%), and some fat (20 to 25%).

Swim meets can last for hours. This prevents normal eating. You don't want to eat a heavy meal or snack because it can make you feel full or sluggish. Small, easily digestible carbohydrate snacks should be your primary choice. Keep the fiber and fat content low at this time.

Avoid caffeine containing drinks, such as tea, coffee, and colas right before and after matches. These drinks can cause further fluid reduction by increasing urine production. Drink enough fluids throughout the day so urine is a light, pale yellow color before the meet starts.

After the meet swimmers should have carbohydrates within 15 to 30 minutes. Adding a little protein at this time will help with the rebuilding and recovery process. Within a couple of hours replace 100 to 150% of the fluid lost or around 15 to 20 ounces per pound of weight lost during play.

Track and Field

"I was told over and over again that I would never be successful, that I was not going to be competitive and the technique was simply not going to work. All I could do was shrug and say 'We'll just have to see'."
—*Dick Fosbury; Olympic Gold Medalist after inventing a revolutionary high-jump technique*

Track meets usually last for hours with a lot of waiting around in between events and heats. Track meets have many different events. In general, the training diet should include: high complex carbohydrates (55 to 60% of total calorie intake), protein (15 to 25%), and some fat (20 to 25%). Carbohydrates are the primary fuel source for all events. Carbohydrates are protein sparing and are needed for recovery. Protein is necessary to maintain muscle and enhance recuperation. Essential fats round out a good athletic diet.

In between events you should have small carbohydrate snacks and sports drinks to maintain fuel supplies and avoid dehydration. Athletes who have good nutrition habits will perform at their best during a meet.

Long-distance athletes need to think more about ways to replenish their fluids and fuel. Short-distance athletes should focus on refueling. Dehydration is less a factor however, fluids should still be replaced as multiple heat events could tap into your reserves. Field-event athletes will focus more on replenishing their used carbohydrates.

You still should avoid caffeine containing drinks, such as tea, coffee, and colas right before and after matches. Further fluid reduction can occur by increasing urine production. Drink enough fluids throughout the day so urine is a light, pale yellow color before starting a match. Athletes should try to drink every 15 to 20 minutes during play.

After the meet athletes should have carbohydrates within 15 to 30 minutes. Adding a little protein at this time will help with the rebuilding and recovery process. Within a couple of hours replace 100 to 150% of the fluid lost or around 15 to 20 ounces per pound of weight lost during play.

Dancing

Dancing is a sport. There I said it. Sure there are no points scored. Well there is in ballroom dancing. But the training and discipline it takes to be a dancer is tremendous. I doubt that many of the top basketball, baseball, or football players could hang. Not that they have to or want to but essentially the training of the serious dancer is at an extreme high level. People just don't think of it that way. That's because the great dancers make it look effortless. Looks can be deceiving.

Nutrition is very important for the dancer. It can be tough to maintain a certain body weight, train, and eat enough food to recuperate from training. Dance can be just as tough mentally.

Believe it or not dance has many similarities to wrestling and boxing. To be successful in these sports you have to be in fantastic condition. You also have to watch your weight. The dancer needs to be able to deliver combinations of powerful moves with skill and grace. (Experienced boxers and wrestlers will feel the same about their sports.) The grace part comes from correct training and possibly genetics (picking the right parents!). The power and strength come from training and also recuperation from correct nutrition and rest. Having the proper nutrition will allow you to energize your muscles allowing them to move swiftly and deliver strong, commanding performances.

Dancing your best requires that your body be properly fueled for classes, rehearsals, and performance. The primary problem with most dancers (just like other athletes) is they just don't eat enough. A diet that is too low in calories will leave the dancer without fuel to function well. The dancing diet should be high in complex carbohydrates (55-60% of total calorie intake), protein (15-20%), and in fat (15-25%).

Like other athletes carbs are the number one fuel source for dancers. Without sufficient carbs the dancer will get tired and fatigue easily during rehearsals or classes. If rehearsals suffer so will performances.

Dancers should eat small sized meals/snacks every 3-4 hours. This will help control appetite, keep the body fueled and reduce chances of over eating. I do realize that someone out there will skip some meals. That in mind dancers should understand that they have 3 "most important" meals. The first is breakfast. Breakfast should never be skipped. Your body has been in a "fasting" state for several hours. You body needs to be fed! The next important meal is your pre-rehearsal/class/performance meal. This should be about 2-3 hours before you start warming up. Carbs are the primary food source. Having too much protein or fat will slow digestion. The last thing you need to feel is bloated on stage!

During your classes and rehearsals drink fluids to stay hydrated (see the *Filling the Gas Tank* chapter). Don't drink too many caffeinated drinks or sodas. The caffeine-laced drinks may help develop a dehydrated state. The sodas may make you feel bloated. There is nothing wrong with drinking sodas but there is a time and a place.

After rehearsals it's important to have some carbohydrates with a little protein to replenish energy stores for full recovery. This will allow the body to take full advantage of the nutritional window of opportunity for recuperation and rebuilding.

Dancing can be fiercely competitive between dancers. It doesn't become a "team" until all the auditions are over. Keeping your body in its best condition physically, mentally, and nutritionally is required for optimal success.

Marching Band

Football players aren't the only athletes on the field in the hot August sun. The marching band should be treated like the athletes they are. The band not only performs at high levels during football games but many participate in marching band competitions. These athlete-musicians obviously practice their musical pieces thoroughly for each performance. But what is misunderstood is the amount of physical effort it takes to perform. They participate in exhaustive training routines. Routines include amazing line formations and complex "plays" on the field. This is done while delivering the goods with an instrument! Band members like other athletes, need a good understanding of nutrition. A good nutrition plan will maximize performance during practice, special events and competitions.

The bands' diet should consist of about 55-60% carbohydrate, 12-15% protein, and 20-30% fat. Carbs are the major energy source used by the muscles. Band members who do not eat enough carbohydrate in their diet will feel more fatigued during classes and rehearsals.

Dehydration is the thing the band has to worry about the most (see the *Filling the Gas Tank* chapter). Dehydration begins after a water loss of only 2%. This can easily happen during game preparation or band competition. Dehydration can affect your practice quality in less than an hour. This can happen sooner if you start practice a little dehydrated. And this is with only a 2% loss. It doesn't take much to lose 2%. This can happen on the field or even if you are sick in bed with the flu vomiting or having bouts of diarrhea.

Early symptoms of dehydration include headaches, dry eyes, drowsiness, loss of concentration, and irritability. Muscle cramps are also a sign of poor fluid replacement. Dehydration of more than three percent of your weight increases the risk of heat illness (see the *Heat Illness, Hyponatrimia, and Cramps, Oh My!* chapter). During practice take water breaks around every 15-20 minutes. Weigh yourself afterwards. Drink about 2 cups of fluids for every pound of body weight lost.

Sports drinks are great to quench thirst and decrease the chances of dehydration. A word of warning here if you have to blow into your instrument. After drinking any sports drink be sure to thoroughly rinse your mouth with water. This will help protect your instrument against any sports drink residue.

After field sessions it's important to have a snack of carbohydrate and a little protein to replenish your energy stores for full recovery.

Cheerleading

Plain and simple: Cheerleading is a sport. It isn't as much a popularity contest like the old days. These are real teams. There are even cheerleading teams that have no school affiliation! And in competition points are scored, trophies won, and scholarships earned. The training and discipline it takes to be a cheerleader is incredible. I know that many of the top basketball, baseball, or football players could not deal with the conditioning of the modern day cheerleader.

Nutrition is very important for the cheerleader. It can be tough to maintain a certain body weight, train, and have enough food to recuperate.

Cheerleading has similarities to gymnastics, wrestling and boxing. For success in these sports you have to be in great condition. You also have to watch your weight. The cheerleader needs to be able to deliver combinations with skill, grace, and power. With a smile! Part of this comes from proper training and part from picking the right parents (genetics). The power and strength come from training and also from full recuperation by way of nutrition and rest.

Cheerleading requires that your body be properly fueled for practice and performance. The major dilemma with most cheerleaders (like a lot of other athletes) is they just don't eat enough. And not enough of the right things. A diet that is too low in calories will leave the cheerleader without fuel to function well or recuperate fully. The cheerleading diet should be high in complex carbohydrates (55-60% of total calorie intake), moderate in protein (15-25%), and fat (15-25%).

Like other athletes, carbohydrates are the primary fuel source for cheerleaders. Without sufficient carbs the cheerleader will get tired and fatigue early during practice. If your practice suffers so will your performance.

Cheerleaders should eat small sized meals/snacks every 3-4 hours. This will help to keep the body fueled and control appetite. Cheerleaders should understand that they have 3 "main meals". The first is breakfast. Breakfast should never be avoided. Your body has been in a "fasting" state for a number of hours. Your mind might be sluggish in the morning but your body is screaming to be fed! The next important meal is your pre-practice or pre-performance meal. This should be about 2-3 hours before you begin warm-ups. Carbs should be the primary food source. Too much protein or fat at this time will slow down digestion. The last thing you need is to feel or look stuffed on stage!

During practice drink some fluids to avoid dehydration (see the *Filling the Gas Tank* chapter). Don't drink caffeinated drinks or sodas. The caffeine-laced drinks can help develop a dehydrated state. The sodas can bloat you like puffer fish. There is nothing wrong with drinking sodas but there is a time and a place.

After practice it's important to have some carbohydrates with a little protein to replenish your energy stores for full recovery. This will allow the body to take full advantage of the natural nutritional window of opportunity for recuperation.

Cheerleading can be intensely competitive among cheerleaders. You'd better be at your best physically, mentally, and nutritionally.

Extreme Sports

Extreme sports include skateboarding, inline skating, mixed martial arts, and much, much more. I haven't figured out why these are so "extreme". Sure there is a rush so to speak. But there's one in just about any sport. It seems that the difference between "regular" sports and "extreme" sports is part individualism, part hype and part marketing. It can be described as a subculture not only relating to the activity but to the type of music shared and clothing worn. The skaters and boarders (on asphalt or snow) could theoretically perform better in compression garments because of the freedom of movement. I bet if you brought this up you'd get very few takers. It just isn't to "cool". Just wait until some ambitious live wire, not caring about what he or she looks like comes out in a bright yellow compression suit and nails everything. You'll start seeing new things on the tour and perhaps in the malls.

Nutrition should be extremely significant for the extreme athlete. To be successful in these sports you have to be in great condition. Or you should be. It all depends on how serious you want to take it. If you put on your skates a couple of times week and try to jump a few stairs you won't get much better. Sure you may improve a little but chances are you'll eat the ground a lot. The guys with the endorsements didn't do it once or twice a week. Some may have eaten properly (not the ground) and some maybe not, but all the top performers put in the time. To get to the next level you have to leave your present level: physically, mentally, and nutritionally.

You may need to watch your weight. You won't get much air if you are too heavy. In some cases the extreme athlete needs to be able to deliver powerful moves with skill and perhaps a little grace. Having the proper nutrition will energize the muscles allowing quick movements and imposing performances.

Performing your best requires that your body be properly fueled. The primary problem with many athletes is they just don't eat enough. The general athletic diet should be high in complex carbohydrates (55-60% of total calorie intake), moderate in protein (15-25%), and fat (15-20%).

Carbohydrates are the primary fuel source for athletes. Without enough carbs you'll get tired easily. You should eat small sized meals/snacks every 3-4 hours. This will help keep the body fueled and ready to go.

The thing extremers have to worry about the most is dehydration (see the *Filling the Gas Tank* chapter). You can begin to get dehydrated after losing only 2% of water. This can easily happen outside on hot humid days. Dehydration can affect your performance in less than an hour. This can happen even sooner if you're already a little dried up from the day before. And this is only with a 2% loss. It doesn't take much to lose 2%. Early symptoms of dehydration include headaches, dry eyes, drowsiness, loss of concentration, and irritability. Muscle cramps are also a sign of poor fluid replacement and electrolyte loss. Dehydration of more than three percent of your weight increases the risk of heat illness (see the *Heat Illness, Hyponatrimia, and Cramps, Oh My!* chapter). Take water breaks around every 15-20 minutes. Weigh yourself after you train. Drink about 2 cups of fluids for every pound of body weight lost. Sports drinks are great to quench thirst and decrease the chances of dehydration.

Stuff You Don't Need but May Find Interesting

Nutrition Almanac, Fifth Edition, McGraw-Hill; 2001.
Lavon J. Dunne

Anatomy of an Illness as Perceived by the Patient: Reflections on Healing and Regeneration. Norman Cousins, New York: WW Norton, 1979.

Nutrient Timing: The Future of Sports Nutrition, John Ivy, Robert Portman, Basic Health Publications, 2004.

Why Do Men Have Nipples? Hundreds of Questions You'd Only Ask a Doctor After Your Third Martini, Mark Leyner, Billy Goldberg MD, Three Rivers Press, 2005.

The Performance Zone: Your Nutrition Action Plan for Greater Endurance & Sports Performance, John Ivy, Robert Portman Basic Health Publications, 2004.

Maximum Performance: Sports Medicine for Endurance Athletes, Michael J. Ross, MD. VeloPress, 2003.

Nutrition for Serious Athletes, Dan Benardot Human Kinetics Publishers, 2000.

Brown L, Rimm EB, Seddon JM, et al. A prospective study of carotenoid intake and risk of cataract extraction in US men. Am J Clin Nutr 1999; 70:517-24.

Cho E, Seddon JM, Rosner B, Willett WC, Hankinson SE. Prospective study of intake of fruits, vegetables, vitamins, and carotenoids and risk of age-related maculopathy. Archives of Ophthalmology 2004; 122:883-92.

Krinsky NI, Landrum JT, Bone RA. Biologic mechanisms of the protective role of lutein and zeaxanthin in the eye. Annu Rev Nutr 2003; 23:171-201.

Escobedo LG, Marcus SE, Holtzman D, Giovino GA. Sports participation, age at smoking initiation, and the risk of smoking among US high school students. JAMA, March 17, 1993; 269:1391-1395.

Antonio J, Uelmen J, Rodriguez R, Earnest C.The effects of Tribulus terrestris on body composition and exercise performance in resistance-trained males. Int J Sport Nutr Exerc Metab. 2000 Jun; 10(2): 208-15.

Bell, D.G., I. Jacobs, and K. Ellerington (2001). Effect of caffeine and ephedrine ingestion on anaerobic exercise performance. *Med. Sci. Sports Exerc.* 33:1399-1403

Mahady, G., C. Gyllenhaal, H. Fong, and N.R. Farnswoth (2000). Ginsengs: a review of safety and efficacy. *Nutr. Clin. Care.* 3:90-101.

King, D.S, R.L. Sharp, M.D. Vukovich, G.A. Brown, T.A. Reifenrath, N.l. Uhl, and K.A. Parsons (1999). Effect of oral androstenedione on serum testosterone and adaptations to resistance training in young men. JAMA 281:2020-2028.

Lemon, PW. (1991). Protein and amino acid needs of the strength athlete. Int. J. Sport Nutr. 1:127-145.

Volek, J. S., Kraemer, W. J., Bush, J. A., Boetes, M., Incledon, T., Clark, K. L., and J. M. Lynch (1997). Creatine supplementation enhances muscular performance during high-intensity resistance exercise. J. Am. Diet. Assoc. 97:765-770.

Volek, J.S., and W.J. Kraemer (1996). Creatine supplementation: Its effect on human muscular performance and body composition. J. Strength Cond. Res. 10:200-210.

Nielsen, F.H., C.D. Hunt, L.M. Mullen, and J.R. Hunt (1987). Effect of dietary boron on mineral, estrogen, and testosterone metabolism in postmenopausal women. FASEB J. 1: 394-397.

Lefavi, R.G., R.A. Anderson, R.E. Keith, G.D. Wilson, J.L. McMillan, and M.H. Stone (1992). Efficacy of chromium supplementation in athletes: emphasis of anabolism. Int. J. Sport Nutr. 2: 111-122.

Lambert, M. I., J. A. Hefer, R.P. Millar, and P.W. Macfarlane (1993). Failure of commercial oral amino acid supplements to increase serum growth hormone concentrations in male body-builders. Int. J. Sports Med. 3:298-305.

American College of Sports Medicine (1996). Position stand on exercise and fluid replacement. *Med. Sci. Sports Exerc.* 28:i-vii.

Adrogué, H.J., and N.E. Madias (2000). Hyponatremia. *New Engl. J. Med.* 342:1581-1589.

Below P.R., R. Mora-Rodriguez, J. Gonzalez-Alonso, E.F. Coyle. Fluid and carbohydrate ingestion independently improve performance during 1h of intense exercise. *Medicine and Science in Sports and Exercise:* Vol. 27, No. 2:200-210, 1995.

Carrithers, J., D. Williamson, P. Gallagher, M. Godard, K. Schulze, S. Trappe. Effects of post exercise carbohydrate-protein feedings on muscle glycogen restoration. *J. Appl. Physiol.* 88:1976-1982, 2000.

Willett W, Manson J, Liu S. Glycemic index, glycemic load, and risk of type 2 diabetes. Am J Clin Nutr 2002; 76:274S-80S

Kris-Etherton PM, Harris WS, Appel LJ. Fish consumption, fish oil, omega-3 fatty acids, and cardiovascular disease. Circulation 2002; 106:2747-57

Haupt, H.A. Anabolic steroids and growth hormone. Am. J. Sports Med. 21(3): 468-474, 1993

The Complete Idiot's Guide to Glycemic Index Weight Loss, Lucy Beale and Joan Clark, Alpha, 2005.

About the Author

Bill Jones is a sought-after sports physical therapist with years of experience helping athletes in their training, physical therapy and nutritional needs. He is an author, certified sports nutritionist and specializes in orthopedics and spine therapy. He has also been a certified personal trainer, certified strength and conditioning specialist, and licensed massage therapist. Bill is a former bodybuilder turned martial artist turned marathoner and lives his advice.

978-0-595-38740-3
0-595-38740-3

Printed in the United States
77455LV00004B/37